Your Body Knows How to Heal

Your Body Knows How to Heal

A Woman's Guide to Preventing and Reversing Heart Disease

Dr. Melissa Samartano, PhD, LMHC, RYT

Published by
Hybrid Global Publishing
301 E 57th Street, 4th fl
New York, NY 10022

Copyright © 2019 by Melissa Samartano

All rights reserved. No part of this book may be reproduced or transmitted in any form or by in any means, electronic or mechanical, including photocopying, recording, or by any information storage and retrieval system, without the written permission of the Publisher, except where permitted by law.

Manufactured in the United States of America, or in the United Kingdom when distributed elsewhere.

Samartano, Melissa
Your Body Knows How to Heal:
A Woman's Guide to Preventing and Reversing Heart Disease
LCCN: 2019907847
ISBN: 9781948181570
eBook: 9781948181587

Cover design by: Natasha Clawson
Cover photo by: Cathleen Broderick
Interior design: Medlar Publishing Solutions Pvt Ltd., India
Photo credits: Cathleen Broderick
Permission credits: If any

http://drsamartano.com/

Disclaimer:
Some names and identifying details have been changed to protect the privacy of individuals.

DEDICATION

May this book bring healing to your heart; not just your physical heart, but also your metaphysical heart. I hope this offering will help you see just how beautiful and magnificent you truly are inside and out. You are worth every minute of commitment to your healing process. You *can* change your life and heal your mind, body, and spirit.

I dedicate this book to my mother Barbara Samartano who passed away from Alzheimer's Disease on July 1, 2019.

There is no relationship like the one we have with our mothers. My mother was my biggest supporter, cheering me on, always looking out for me and loving me no matter what non-traditional way I chose to live my life.

My mother taught me to always stand up for myself, fight for what's right and help others in need. I would not be where I am today without her unconditional love as a mother, support as a parent, wisdom from heaven and grace from God.

With infinite love and light,

Your Daughter

CONTENTS

Introduction   ix

Chapter 1:   The Current State of Affairs   1
Chapter 2:   The Role of Stress   17
Chapter 3:   The Psychology of Heart Disease   35
Chapter 4:   Eating for Heart Health   51
Chapter 5:   Exercise for Heart Health   69
Chapter 6:   Lifestyle Changes for a Healthier Heart   91
Chapter 7:   The Missing Link for True Heart Health   109
Chapter 8:   Fine-Tune Your Program   123
Chapter 9:   Trust the Healing Process   137

Acknowledgments   145
Notes   147

INTRODUCTION

TRYING TO DO IT ALL ON YOUR OWN CAN COST YOU EVERYTHING

If you ask the average person, "What is the deadliest disease for women?" most people will reply, "Breast cancer" without even missing a beat. While it's great that we have raised our collective awareness of breast cancer, this average response fails to address the elephant in the room: breast cancer isn't even close to being the number one killer of women. That distinction belongs to heart disease. Heart disease is responsible for one out of every three deaths in women. In fact, heart disease kills more women than *all other cancers combined*. It also kills significantly more women than it does men. And yet, as a woman, you hardly hear about heart disease in the news or even at the doctor's office. Which is a devastating shame, because not being aware of your own heart health can cost you everything.

Why? Why are women so prone to heart problems?

Many people will point to the typical American diet of salty, fatty, processed foods. And yes, nutrition absolutely plays an important role. But in my twenty years of counseling, and in my own struggles with heart disease, I have a deeper view of the problem.

If you think about it, a woman is a lot like a heart: she never stops. You can depend on her to keep going no matter what. She is consistently, without fail, pumping out the love, compassion, and energy that her loved ones—and the world—need to keep going.

As women, we have such loving, giving hearts. Our heart is definitely the source of our super powers. Driven by the generosity of our hearts, we often take on so much: having kids, volunteering, pursuing a career, and being the emotional rock for our partners, families, and friends. Truly, our capacity to take care of business and of others is a force of nature! And yet, trying to do it all without feeling like you have the same love and support coming back to you that you send out to others, can overtax your heart.

In my holistic therapy practice, I sit across from women every day who are struggling. A full 90 percent of them are so stressed it's taking a toll on their heart health. Whether it's their physical heart, and they now require blood pressure medication and/or a daily aspirin, or it's their metaphorical heart and they're feeling overwhelmed, unsupported, and completely emotionally exhausted. Many of them are on antidepressants instead of, or in addition to, their heart medications. And yet, whatever medication they've been given, they don't feel any better.

It's no wonder they're feeling so worn out. The women I work with are doing it all; they are the hub of their family's wheel, attending to everyone's needs before their own. They often work in high-stress jobs. Perhaps one of their children has special needs. Or maybe one is in a relationship that doesn't feel as supportive as they'd like; it may even be dysfunctional. Whatever their particular circumstances are, these women often feel like there's no chance for rest, no time when they don't need to be getting things done. They are worn out emotionally and physically. Typically, there is some troubling symptom that is starting to clamor for their attention. It could be a racing heartbeat or high blood pressure. Maybe it's dizziness or the inability to sleep because they can't turn down their whizzing thoughts.

They are desperate for relief, for some sensation of peace, no matter how fleeting. The fact that their heart is starting to show signs of strain is only heightening their urgent need for relief, and thus making their stress, the source of the problem, worse.

A simple truth underlies our desire to help others and the state of depletion so many of us find ourselves in, and it's that you can't give from an empty cup. For so many of us women, our cups are bone dry.

If you can identify, I want you to know that no matter who you are, what you're dealing with, or how sick you may feel, you can heal your heart and your life. I know this because I have been the one at the doctor's office with a stress-related heart condition (in my case, a dangerously high heart rate). I went down the path of traditional medicine to find a cure, but in the end I healed myself. I did it by learning powerful, scientifically-proven tools that promote heart health: nutrition, exercise, relaxation, and psychological tools that support the body and the mind, and create all the conditions our bodies need to function their best. Over the course of twenty years in my clinical counseling practice, I've helped thousands of others do it, too. Now it's your turn.

Two Surgeries, Ten Days in the ICU, and Twenty Years Ago

I know exactly how these women feel, and how you are likely feeling, too; no matter how hard you work or fast you go, you are still barely keeping it together.

Early in my career, I was working in a high-stakes job with a two-hour commute each way. I was pouring everything into my work, fueling myself with coffee to compensate for my exhaustion. On the weekends, I was drinking too much wine and not eating enough food in general. I was definitely not eating enough healthy foods to provide the nutrients necessary to empower my body to prevent disease and manage stress. I figured I was young and resilient enough to muddle through, but my body had other ideas.

I developed ventricular tachycardia, a heart rhythm disorder characterized by an irregular and rapid heart rate caused by abnormal electrical signals in the ventricles, which are the lower chambers of the heart. If not treated, the disorder can increase the risk of stroke, sudden cardiac arrest, and possibly death. My heart rate would periodically surge as high as

300 beats per minute for 45 minutes at a time, which is astoundingly high when you consider that a typical at-rest heart rate is closer to 70. I was losing consciousness and fainting regularly, ending up in the emergency room most weekends and calling in sick to work. With a heart rate that high, I could have had a heart attack or stroke and died at any given moment.

I spent so much time in the doctor's office. Their best suggestion was to perform an ablation on my heart. They inserted a catheter into an artery in my groin, and a device then stimulated my heart muscle in the specific area they thought was causing the abnormal heart rhythm. The chief of cardiology at Rhode Island Hospital performed this procedure twice to find the areas of my heart where he felt the electrical current was going awry. After the first ablation didn't work, he tried a second one. My stress levels were dangerously high from my job, long commute, and generally being in a transitional place in my life, so the ablations failed to fix the problem. I continued to end up in the ER most weekends, and even spent ten days in the intensive care unit. Nothing seemed to be helping my heart stay in a normal range.

Finally, I had to admit that traditional doctors and hospitals weren't helping. I went off my meds, told my doctor I wasn't going to come back, and started booking acupuncture appointments. After my third appointment with the acupuncturist, I saw a significant difference in my stress levels. I went home after that appointment and slept for a day and a half. My fiancé was so worried about me, but I needed the rest. My parasympathetic nervous system (which you'll learn more about in Chapter 2) got stimulated, which triggered a healing response in my body. That was the turning point for me.

I kept going to acupuncture, got back into doing yoga, started meditating, and cleaned up my diet. Through my meditation practice, I reconnected to a power greater than myself. I started benefiting from inspirational insights and a general feeling of support from life itself. I stopped feeling like I had to figure everything out on my own.

I quit my job and never looked back. Even more importantly, I recalibrated who I was. I decided to go back to school to get my PhD in holistic counseling so that I could help others learn the techniques that saved my life. I became a licensed mental health counselor (LMHC) in the state of Massachusetts and eventually opened the Holistic Counseling Center in Raynham, Massachusetts. In other words, I started following my heart.

And you know what? It worked. My condition evaporated. I went back to my cardiologist a year later, just to tell him how well I was doing. He told me he had been concerned about my choices back then, but he could now see how well I was doing. He also said that I could help a lot of people by sharing my story. Even to this day, I haven't needed to go back to see him. I had to get to the point where I decided that I wasn't going to wait anymore for medicine and doctors to fix my problem. I was going to put together a treatment plan and course of action that spoke to my heart. And in doing so, I gave my body what it needed to heal itself.

Through my personal experience, my years of training, and my decades of counseling women, I have put together a guide comprising all the tools I used to help myself, and the tools that have helped countless others heal their hearts as well. The result is what you're holding in your hands right now.

This book is for you if:

- You give, and you give, and you give, but you don't seem to have the time to do the things that you know replenish you, whether that's taking a walk with a girlfriend, pursuing a hobby, crawling into bed early with a great book, having down time with your partner, or even getting to the gym.
- You run on caffeine to keep yourself going, and on processed foods that require little preparation so you can feed yourself with minimal time. Perhaps you perk yourself up in the afternoon with some chocolate, a pastry, or a Frappuccino.
- You've gone to see your primary care physician to tell him or her how tired you feel, how overwhelmed you are, or how you feel stressed all the time. And you've left with a prescription for Lexapro, hoping that will help. When that doesn't work, you tried

another medication. Then another. When none of those made you feel much better, your hopes got dashed.
- Your body has developed some troubling symptoms that are negatively impacting how you feel, and perhaps even scaring you.
- You know there's got to be a better way, but darned if you know what it is.

This book is that better way. What you're holding can show you exactly what you need to do to give yourself a palpable sense of relief and help you give yourself the support you're craving. It will help you see the patterns passed down through your family that have been contributing to how hard your life has been feeling. You'll learn how to give yourself space to feel your feelings so that you can unburden your heart. You'll see the simple nutritional shifts you can make and exercises you can do to support your body and give it what it needs to be able to heal the particular health challenges you are facing. And it will help you develop a plan you enjoy and can commit to that will help you create the physiological state of relaxation needed for your body to be able to heal itself.

How to Use This Book

Every time I start to work with a new patient, I walk them through the same process, which is exactly what I teach in this book. I wish that I could somehow magically work with all the people who need this information one-on-one. It is such an honor to work with my clients. They learn to see where their stress is coming from and how they can choose better responses to it. We get on the yoga mat and they experience profound relaxation, often for the first time in years. They slowly come off their meds. Their lives stabilize, their relationships improve, and they even start to do things in their personal lives or in their career that are more meaningful to them simply because they have the bandwidth now to try new things. All these results stem from the course of action that is in this book.

The information contained on these pages combines the best of the Western and Eastern approaches to heart health, both physical and emotional. In these pages, I've combined the science behind nutrition, exercise, stress relief, and the healing response with Western psychology—theories developed by Freud that help objectively identify patterns, as well as techniques, from cognitive behavioral therapy to rewrite those patterns.

From the Eastern world, I've included the practices of meditation, yoga, affirmations, and the energetic body to help you find health on a physiological, psychological, and spiritual level. Because I wrote my PhD dissertation on using yoga poses and the chakras to heal the body and the mind, this is one of my favorite portions of the work I do with clients, but all the pieces play an important role and add up to a cohesive whole.

At the end of each chapter you'll learn a specific tool for you to try, whether it's a strategy for changing negative thoughts, bolstering yourself with affirmation, or a breathing technique that will help you sleep. The more you actually do the things you discover in this book—and not just read about them—the more progress you'll make, and the more quickly you'll make it, even if you're really struggling and feeling hopeless.

No matter your age or your circumstance, you deserve to feel good in your body and your mind. To do this, you've got to treat yourself well. The only person who is currently preventing you from feeling and being treated better is you. I can give you recommendations and guidance, but you have to make the changes. And when you do make those changes, you can absolutely lead a happier, healthier life, no matter how severe your illness is or how chaotic your circumstances may be.

In order to start feeling better, there are three things you have to do:

- You have to actually develop a plan and take action based on what you read in this book. Even though your thoughts and

emotions have great power, only by taking different actions will you create different results.
- You have to be patient with the process. Healing yourself takes time. But you know what? Western medicine takes time, too. Just as it takes time to fully recover from a broken bone or surgery, it also takes time to heal your heart.
- Finally, you have to trust in the healing process. Believing that you can improve your own health is key. And if it feels inaccessible at this point, know that I'll give you the science and the true stories from my own life, and the lives of my patients, to help you access that trust.

Your body is your most powerful ally and partner. You only have to empower it. I know you're not perfect. No one is. But there is a path that is ideal for you that you can only perfect by starting to take one step after the other. Just as it is true that your stressors and your reactions to those stressors have contributed to your current state of illness, it is also true that you can choose new reactions and create a new state of health.

It is an indisputable truth that your body is brilliantly wired for health. You just have to give it what it needs to get back to balance. The things I'm referring to aren't secret, or particularly hard. Many of them, such as the nutrition tips I'll share, are common sense. Others, like the meditations and yoga poses I'll teach you, have been around for thousands of years, passed down from generation to generation. And today is the day this transformative information gets handed over to you. On these pages, I'll show you exactly what your heart needs to keep doing its vital work of keeping you alive and connected to others, and I'll walk you through how to give yourself those things that support your heart. The tools I'll share are real solutions, based on real science, that have worked for countless real people.

I know there's probably a voice in your head right now that's saying, "They may work for other people, but not for me." And I want you to let it in when I say, the strategies in this book can work for you, too—all you need to do is practice them and trust the process.

I've had the honor of seeing countless people with huge obstacles in their path use these tools to change their health and their lives for the better. It's great if you have a therapist or another health-care provider to guide you, but you don't have to go sit on someone's couch or examination table to put these tools into place. That's exactly why I'm writing this book; as much as I love my work, I can't work one-on-one with everyone who needs help. I keep hiring clinicians to increase the number of people we can help, but still my practice is at overcapacity. And when I think back to my own journey, I see that I did most of it myself, with only the help of a few important teachers and books to guide me. That's what I hope this book will be able to do for you, to give you the guidance and the inspiration you need to heal yourself on your own, too.

CHAPTER 1

THE CURRENT STATE OF AFFAIRS

Let's say it took you fifteen minutes to read this far into this book. In those fifteen minutes, fifteen women died from a complication related to heart disease. That is how vulnerable we are to physical issues with our hearts.

And yet, you hear very little about the risks of heart disease for the female population. Why don't we hear more about the perils of heart disease for women? When heart disease first came into the public eye in a big way it was the mid-1950s, and President Eisenhower had a heart attack. His doctors recommended he start exercising and stop eating red meat, and media everywhere took up the cause to promote dietary and lifestyle changes for men. But why was the information and the concern focused primarily on men?

The fact is, while women have come a long way, we have to battle a perception and a reality that we don't matter as much as men. (Talk about a heartbreaker!) While we are changing out of the old pattern of living in a male-centric world, this perception is still very much alive.

In the medical field, there is copious research and personal stories of doctors not listening to women as they describe their symptoms, telling them it's all in their heads. Women haven't been the subject of research studies to the extent that men have, not by a long shot. In fact, a 2016 study found that even though women make up more than half of the post-doctoral population of neuroscientists, fewer than 22 percent of the lead authors of peer-reviewed studies in this area are women.[1]

The sad truth is if a medical finding isn't about men or written by a man, it's not viewed as important and receives less attention. I'm sure you've seen photos of Senate committee meetings to discuss health care, which is as much a woman's concern as a man's, yet all the participants in the room are men. All the more reason for us women to take our heart health into our own hands.

It's not just the field of medicine where women are underrepresented. In 2019, women made up only about 24 percent of the U.S. Congress,[2] 28 percent of state legislators,[3] and 18 percent of governors.[4] In corporate America, women hold only 23 percent of senior executive posts, and only 4 percent of CEO roles.[5]

Frankly, few people are talking about women's heart health because the people steering the conversation are men. It's time we take our heart health into our own hands, for our own sakes, as well as for the benefit of our mothers, sisters, friends, daughters, and granddaughters. To do just that, let's take a closer look at the risk factors that are hiding just under our noses. If you want to address a systemic problem, you've got to understand it first. So, let's get to the heart of the matter. At its root, women's heart disease is the result of the stresses of the modern world.

The Role of External Stressors

I know that you picked up this book because you want *remedies* to the stressors that contribute to heart disease in women, not because you want to spend more time thinking about those stressors. You probably feel like you already know all you ever want to know about stressors, because you're living with them every day. But I think you will find it eye-opening to take an objective look at just how many reasons there are that so many of our hearts are feeling more taxed than ever before.

I also want to be real with you; even though I have so many relaxation-promotion tools at my disposal, I understand just how stressful life is for the vast majority of us. My husband and I don't even have kids, although we did recently adopt a puppy, and we can barely keep up with all of the demands on our plate! Yesterday, for example, I had to attend a meeting an hour away in Rhode Island regarding my mom who has dementia. When I came into the office later that day, I needed to support a couple of my clinicians in helping with their patients. I saw my own patients back-to-back until 8:00 p.m., and after work I met my husband at the dog-training class for our new puppy. All the while, I was dealing with text messages and emails from people who needed to reschedule their appointments, talking with new referrals who needed an over-the-phone consultation, figuring out which therapists have openings for intakes, as well as reading group texts about the office holiday gathering. And still trying to connect with family about making important decisions for my mother's care, whether moving her to a nursing home facility or keeping her in assisted living care is the next best option for her. I didn't get home until ten o'clock that night, and I was ready to throw my phone out the window. This is just a typical day, reflecting the combination of work and family responsibilities that we all juggle.

My goal in covering these stressors is to show that we women have every reason to feel as stressed as we do, and as a result, to be as prone to heart disease as we are. I want to normalize your experience and help you see the many places stress comes from so that you can stop feeling like there is something wrong with you. Stress is a perfectly natural reaction to very powerful forces, and you are by no means alone in feeling it.

To help raise your awareness of all the ways stress may be creating conditions that are hospitable to disease in your body, here's a brief tour through the contributing stressors most of us face.

A Poor Diet

When I was in my late twenties and working my high-stress job with the two-hour commute, I barely ate at all because I simply didn't dedicate any time to shopping, cooking, or even deciding what to order from a restaurant. I basically ate whatever I could grab. There were no nutrient-rich, whole foods. My go-to eating strategies were picking up a tuna sub, ordering Chinese food, or maybe having a bowl of cereal for dinner.

The quality of a typical American's diet has deteriorated in exact proportion to how available packaged convenience foods have become. I know how tempting it is to grab a bag of something that you can eat in the car on the way to work in the morning so that you can save time. Plus, those foods are generally affordable and manufactured to taste delicious. They're so packed with salt, sugar, and manufactured flavorings that they become addictive and they can change your palate to the point that healthy, whole foods, such as fruits and vegetables, taste bland.

There are entire grocery store aisles filled with various bars: granola bars, protein bars, cereal bars, and nut bars. The thought of taking the time for an actual daytime meal can seem silly, maybe even delusional.

The problem is that the high salt and sugar content of these processed foods are very stressful to the heart. And the level of nutrients that get stripped out during processing means you don't end up giving your body the nutrients it needs to function well. Ironically, your effort to mitigate your stress by saving yourself the time it takes to cook and eat a meal, actually adds to it.

A more insidious reason why we often reach for these packaged, processed, and highly marketed foods is that we buy into the idea that they will help us look a certain way. We want to fit the mold of what our culture tells us women should look like, which is thin, attractive, and put together at all times. In our efforts to meet these expectations, we deprive ourselves of the things we need to be truly healthy and whole. In other words, we sacrifice our heart health for the sake of how others see us.

A Lack of Movement

Our computer-based lives now require us to sit at our desks for hours and hours each day. Add in a commute on top of that, and you can spend up to twelve hours a day sitting—even more than you sleep! The problem is that our bodies, and our hearts, were designed for regular movement. We need physical exertion to strengthen our hearts, to purge stress, and to clear our minds. After all, we evolved to be able to walk upright. It is in our DNA to be on the move. Sitting still is stressful to the body and weakens the heart.

I'm not saying we should all be training for a marathon, or start doing CrossFit seven days a week. But if we never take care of our physical needs, our heart health—as well as our overall physical and emotional health—will suffer, too.

The Stress that Comes from Society at Large

When you read the stats of how women aren't represented equally in the boardroom, the statehouse, or the scientific journals, it's saddening, isn't it? But this sadness is more than a fleeting feeling. I believe that all women in America suffer from under-acknowledged stress and even trauma that comes from the realities of being a woman. And if you're a woman of color, the stress and trauma is even higher. Being a woman makes every task we take on, or accomplishment we achieve, even harder. Not only is that constant labor exhausting, it's also demoralizing. And our heart pays the price.

I own my own business, I have a PhD, and I'm still not respected by men in my field, or even in my own family. I've had to work hard to fight for my voice to be heard. Again and again, I've heard things like, "What do you mean you're going to run a business and not have children?" Men don't have to fight to have a voice and to be respected for their knowledge, experience, and intelligent minds. Even my husband and I are treated differently by our own families; his choices are celebrated while mine are questioned.

While I don't pine for the gender-defined roles of the past, when men were the primary breadwinners and women were the primary caretakers, it is undeniable that everyone had less on their plate when we stuck to our particular domains. Now that women are in the workforce, we have job responsibilities as well as family responsibilities. It leaves us all feeling the pinch, particularly as job hours have steadily expanded due to long commutes and late-night and early-morning email and text check-ins.

As our economy shifts away from manufacturing and more toward information technology, college and even graduate-level education is more important—and more expensive—than ever. With tuition as high as it is, it's becoming more common for people to have high student debt with salaries that aren't high enough to pay it off.

That puts pressure on kids to learn more and do more from a young age so that they're attractive to admissions and scholarship committees. This puts more pressure on parents and kids, and more strain on a marriage to navigate the ever higher hurdles needed to insure success for kids.

Many women are subject to an unspoken coercion, or sometimes, pressure that is vocally expressed by a family member or friend to achieve the education, career, marriage, and kids according to a socially acceptable timeline. When I was in my thirties, I got so much pressure from family and friends to get married and have children. I felt excluded from my friend group simply because I wasn't experiencing these major life moments when they were. I felt very alone. And my family gave me a lot of negative feedback for my life choices. Whenever I said I didn't want to have a baby, they would say, "What's wrong with you?" It created major feelings of disconnection and isolation, both of which are stressful.

My brother, on the other hand, did everything "right." He got married, had kids, and appeared to be living the American dream. It took some defiance and rebellion, and some depression, too, for me to get through that time. Years later, my brother went through a horrible divorce. Many of my friends who got married when we were in our early thirties are now divorced and looking at me saying, "Wow, you did the right thing." But it certainly didn't feel that way when I was living through it.

I can look to my younger friends, who are now in their mid-to-late thirties, and see that they have more choices than I did, and they can talk about those choices so much more openly than I felt I could. I am proud to have helped pave the way for younger generations to feel more confident in making nontraditional life choices. Yet there are many people out there of all ages, and from all cultures, still feeling societal pressure to conform to a typical life.

We're also living through an intense moment in our society with women speaking out about sexual harassment. Although it is ultimately healing to stop keeping secrets, it's also stressful to process the new insights that arise every day. If you have any history of sexual abuse or harassment—a 2018 national survey found that 81 percent of American women have experienced some form of sexual harassment and/or assault[6]—each new revelation can be another trigger. It's a lot to process in a short amount of time. The news cycle can feel relentless, adding not only to the number of issues that need our attention, but also to the emotional upset that a typical day brings. Change of all types is often stressful, and this cultural shift that is moving us toward a healthier climate is tumultuous.

Sexual orientation and gender issues are also coming to light, which again is immensely healing because people don't have to hide who they are any longer. As a culture, we're moving toward openness, but there is often backlash to progress. Sometimes the two steps forward, two steps back nature of social evolution can feel more like whiplash than growth.

Trying to Do It All

Woman are natural born multitaskers, planners, organizers, and doers. These superpowers we have are also double-edged swords. When we take on that extra project at work, say yes to the volunteer requests, spearhead the caregiving of an ill relative or friend, or take the lead in managing the household as well as working a full-time job, we give so much that we get depleted. We run out of energy to give to ourselves. And we take care of others better than we care for ourselves.

Please don't get me wrong, I absolutely believe we can have fulfilling relationships, family lives, financial lives, personal lives, and careers. But we need to give ourselves the chance to rest and recuperate from our exertions. Our physical heart needs that rest, and so does our emotional heart.

Technology and the Pace of Life

It's an undeniable fact that people are working more, and are expected to be in work mode for longer hours than ever before. It's no longer acceptable to return a message within twenty-four hours; people expect you to respond within the hour. We are living an on-demand lifestyle, with texts constantly buzzing, email boxes continually dinging, and social media comments and likes constantly streaming in.

All this connectivity is another huge reason why we are not giving ourselves any time to rest. When I talk to my clients about putting down smartphones at certain times so they can have more downtime, they look at me like I have sprouted horns.

Every notification we receive on our phones is a stressor—even if it bears good news. These little computers we carry around (or perhaps even have strapped to our wrist) are highly addictive and highly stimulating. Using them all day, every day leads to not getting enough rest at night. We watch videos on our phones in bed at night, and then reach for the phone to check emails and texts the moment our eyes open in the morning.

We are never getting a break from the sensory stimulation they provide. We get addicted to it, too. When we have a slow email day, we don't think, "Phew, I can relax." Instead, we think, "What's going on? Is something wrong? Nobody loves me."

Social media is no help for our stress levels, either. They give the appearance of social connection without the benefits of feeling truly supported. It's all too common that a friend will wish you a wonderful birthday on social media, but will walk right past you if they see you at the grocery store (a phenomenon several of my patients have experienced).

There are multiple studies, including one from researchers at the University of Pittsburgh in 2016,[7] that show a significant association between social media usage and depression. It makes sense; because when you go on social media, it is so easy to compare yourself to what you see your peers doing. And make no mistake—your friends aren't sharing their troubles or concerns on social media. We all tend to show the well-edited version of our lives, sharing only the photos and updates that make it look like everything is going great. So when you compare your own life and feel worse about yourself, that comparison is based on a distorted reality. You don't see your friends' dramas or hardships, because they're not going to share something that shows any chinks in their armor. You may remember a particular post you or a friend shared that was real and vulnerable and that got a big response and think, *not all social media posts are unrealistic*. But if it weren't so unusual for someone to share something real on social media, that particular incident wouldn't stick out so much in your mind. Moments of authenticity may indeed happen on social media, but they are the exception, not the rule.

Social media also weakens the real-life relationships we have. If you have a basic understanding of what's happening in a friend's life based on what she chooses to share on social media, you're less likely to reach out for a real conversation. It's so much better to see someone in person, or talk on the phone, than to rely on a comment here and a like there. When you meet in person, you get a hug, you look each other in the eye, and you ask how the other person is really doing. Even if you're talking on the phone you can hear the other person's tone and get a better understanding of her emotional state. Either way, you have a more honest conversation that leads to connection instead of comparison.

When we lose our sense of connection to other people, we lose our real-world support system, which adds another stressor to our lives—humans are social creatures and need a network to thrive.

Our addiction to technology and all the detriments it brings is also starting earlier and earlier. Kids want all the high-tech gadgets they see their parents and peers spending so much time looking at. Adolescents now are FaceTiming with friends instead of getting together or going over to each other's homes. They are in the comfort of their own homes watching movies together through FaceTime. Even in the same room with their friends, kids engage more with their devices than with each other. Adults are often guilty of this too. When we miss our opportunities to connect with each other, we miss the opportunity to release some of our stress. It is vital to our mental health to have people we care about hear and see our feelings.

I always ask my clients: who is your support system? If your parents have dementia, or your kid has ADHD, for example, you need people you can rely on. So many of my clients don't even have a good friend they can turn to. When we feel like we don't have time to nurture good relationships, then we end up feeling isolated; that's when the pressure and stress lead to depression and disease.

Other age-old social stressors include pettiness, judgment, and gossip. When we spend time with a friend or group of friends and the only topic of conversation is gossip, it can make you wonder, *is there anyone I can trust?* It can even lead to a sense of hopelessness.

We need to honor one another, respect each other's choices, and not judge other people. We're all just doing our best. And we're all going to disappoint others at times, because we are all human.

The Economy

With the ever-widening reach of technology, our economy is in flux as well. Companies are frequently reorganizing and downsizing in an effort to stay nimble. As a result, many people are fearful of losing their jobs, or have lost their job. Getting fired or laid off, having to take on more responsibility at work, or changing careers, are all some of the most stressful experiences in a person's life. Every worker has to face these events with more frequency than ever before.

In addition to an unstable job market, the focus on luxury housing and the disappearance of affordable housing has led people to spend a much higher percentage of their income on their home than in decades past. According to the 2017 "The State of the Nation's Housing" published by the Joint Center Housing Studies at Harvard University, thirty-nine million Americans can't afford their homes, and are paying more than 30 percent of their income on housing costs.[8] For so many Americans, money is going less far, just as their ability to make money is more unstable than ever. It's enough to keep you awake at night, wondering and worrying about how to pay your bills.

Constant Transitions

With the increased frequency in changing jobs, a high divorce rate, and a shifting culture, we now experience times of flux much more frequently than people of previous generations did. In the face of transition and the unpredictability it brings, everyone experiences some degree of stress, and some experience more severe symptoms. Don't get me wrong: some instability is good because it can force us to grow and evolve. But when it becomes constant, we lose the ability to rest, recharge, and heal. We are constantly in reaction mode.

Even positive transitions are stressful. Getting married, for example, seems like a peak happiness experience. But learning to go through life as part of a unit, rather than an individual, is a transition that can be very challenging and emotionally upsetting. It may surprise you to hear that getting married is one of the top seven most stressful life events, according to the Holmes-Rahe Life Stress inventory, only slightly less stressful than a major personal illness or injury. Many people don't think about the reality of what it will be like to be married. It's a pipe dream to think that you're going to automatically be happy after you get married. The divorce rates are proof of that.

Having children is the same; children require all kinds of sacrifices, like sleep, money, and time. Those sacrifices can be a real shock and source of stress. It's also more likely now that a child will have a behavior disorder, which adds to parental stress even more. One in fifty-nine children now have autism, according to the Centers for Disease Control and Prevention (CDC),[9] and just under one in ten children have Attention Deficit and Hyperactivity Disorder (ADHD), also according to the CDC.[10]

No matter what stage of life you are in, you are likely going through some kind of major transition or stress:

- **People in their late teens and early twenties** are often seeking to get into college, and find the money to pay for it. After they graduate, they typically have a ton of debt, and fiercely competitive job prospects. Many move back in with their parents to save money until their careers get off the ground, which can be a good money-saver, but also a stressful clash of cultures.
- **People in their mid-twenties** tend to move frequently and change jobs a lot as they find their career groove. It's a time of major transition that can last well into their thirties.
- **People in their thirties** are often getting married and starting families, two life events that are as stressful as they are positive. Even those who aren't married are often in a demanding job that is continually requiring them to upgrade their skills.
- **People in their late thirties, forties, and early fifties** are often caught in what feels like a vise—trying to meet the demands of work and taking care of their kids and parents, all while paying the mortgage and bills.
- **Many people in their sixties and seventies** are finding themselves unable to retire or to vacation in Florida. They likely

didn't save enough, or they may find themselves raising their grandkids.

Infidelity

A full 60 percent of the women I see in my practice are dealing with infidelity. A betrayal of trust is accompanied by emotional pain that weighs heavily on your heart. It's the source of an enormous amount of stress and unhappiness that can lead to illness in the body. Very often you'll see it manifest as heart disease, autoimmune disorders (which are much more likely to affect women than men), or cancer.

After an infidelity, it's common to think, *I can't believe this is happening to me! How is this my life?* You have to face the rumors and people talking about you behind your back.

One of my clients is a beautiful, intelligent woman who looks, from the outside, like she's got it all: adorable children, a loving husband, and a good job. Most people would have looked at her life and been envious. She recently found out her husband had an affair with her best friend. Then she got laid off. This all led her down a path to experiencing panic attacks, anxiety, and an emotional breakdown.

On top of the infidelity, my client was struggling with feelings of isolation because she felt she couldn't talk about what she was experiencing. She told me of how she left a party in tears; everyone was talking about what they would do if they found out their husbands were having an affair, and she felt she couldn't be honest. Any emotional upset you face gets compounded when you feel you have to hide it for fear of judgment.

A betrayal of trust is an emotional trauma to your heart center, which is the origin of your love for yourself, your family, and your community. When the heart center is traumatized, it's crippling. It's hard to open yourself up and love again. The resulting disconnection from others is a further source of stress that kicks off a cycle that too often manifests as heart disease.

Our Emotional Nature

As women—although this does relate to many men, I still consider it more of a female trait—we often have a tendency to harbor negative emotions such as guilt, anger, and shame. Many of us have had an experience where we spoke our truth and someone's feelings got hurt, or someone judged us for it, and we've never forgotten. So, we swallow our truth. We are not honest with other people or even with ourselves.

The problem is that not speaking your mind or listening to your heart is a recipe for heart disease. This tendency to hold on to things is causing harm. Because you've picked up this book, it's high time to set some of those cares down.

This habit of harboring negative emotions also makes it difficult for us to focus on the positive. When I wrote the first draft of this chapter, I typed many paragraphs about how my husband is so much better at establishing boundaries with his family than I am. When I showed him what I wrote, he told me that I am the one who taught him how be in a healthy relationship with them. He pointed out that I taught him how to confront conflict and set healthy limits by strengthening his communication skills. And he told me that if he hadn't met me, he doesn't know if he would have a healthy relationship with his family like he does today.

It really made me stop and think. I realized he's right. It has taken years of work in my own therapy, education, and my practice, but I *have* gotten really good at setting very clear limits and boundaries with my family, and not allowing them to make me feel guilty or bad about myself or my decisions. I also have learned not to care so much about how others feel about me, so they can't manipulate me or guilt me into choices that are not healthy for me.

This experience perfectly exemplifies a dangerous tendency we as women often have; we don't give ourselves credit for the good that we do and the strengths that we bring to the table. As a result, we rarely get that sense of achievement that allows us to feel accomplished and fulfilled. When we don't acknowledge the ground we've taken, and focus only on what's left undone or unsaid, we never get that, "Ahh, I did a good job and now I can relax for a bit" feeling.

Not being honest, not speaking your mind or listening to your heart, and not loving and valuing yourself is a recipe for heart disease. Because you've picked up this book, I know you're hungry for change. Take that desire as all the motivation—and permission—you need to start doing things differently.

Summary

If you are noticing that your body is showing signs of strain from modern life, I want you to know that you are not imagining it. There isn't something wrong with you. You aren't weak. You aren't unlucky. You are living a normal life.

I also share these insights to show you that creating more peace in your life isn't as simple as just removing stressors from your life, although that can be helpful. Unfortunately, stressors are here to stay.

Change is stressful, but it can have a higher purpose. Talking about your stressors and making positive changes in your life will help you and your heart health. Even more amazingly, it will help everyone around you, even globally. Making changes in your life will help you be a healthier and happier being. Allowing other people to see you make changes in your life will help the people around you do the same. Your actions create a lovely and powerful ripple effect, and just by picking up this book and reading this far you have put those ripples into motion.

Let's keep going. In the next chapter, we'll take a look at what happens in the body when you are stressed, and how that impacts your heart. You will learn further information and gain the motivation to use the techniques we'll start covering in Section 2, which will help you change the way you respond to stress. You will learn to spend more time in relaxation so that you balance out your nervous system and build your resilience.

CHAPTER 2

THE ROLE OF STRESS

Now that you've gotten some context on all the ways real life can cause stress, it's time to take a look at how that stress translates into physical disease in the body. This is often a missing link for people. You may have a vague notion that stress is somehow involved in most chronic diseases, but unless you really gain a clearer understanding of how that connection works, you may not be motivated to take the necessary steps to alleviate that stress.

I often talk to clients about specific approaches to creating more calm in their lives, and even though their stress has gotten bad enough to force them to seek out professional help to deal with it, they generally respond to my suggestions with an air of, "Yeah, yeah, yeah, I'll do that someday." Or, the look in their eyes tells me that what we're discussing may sound like good ideas, but there just isn't enough time in the day to do them. Sometimes, a little bit of objective knowledge and a few simple steps are just the ticket to get you to do things differently. I hope that's what this chapter will do.

How Stress Self-Perpetuates

When something catches on fire, you know that in order to put it out you want to either douse it in water or smother it with a blanket to cut off the oxygen. And you probably also know that the last thing you want to do is to pour gasoline on the fire because that will only make the fire a lot bigger and more out of control. Stress is a lot like fire. A little bit of it is okay (nothing like the anticipation of a deadline to spur you into action, after all), but if you want to extinguish it when it gets to be too much, you have to choose the right tools or else you will only make the stress worse.

Based on the hundreds of people who walk through my practice door every month, I can tell you that most of us do the equivalent of throwing gasoline on our stress fires by choosing coping mechanisms that make stress bigger and more harmful, like an out of control fire. In order to reduce your stress, you need to understand what makes it worse, what makes it better, and how you've typically been reacting to it. With just a little bit of insight and awareness, you can start responding to stress effectively so that your experience of it is lessened, and so that you create the conditions that your body needs to heal and your inner wisdom needs to be heard.

In this chapter, you'll come to understand the toll stress can take on the body in general, especially the heart, as well as how you choose to respond to that stress can make that toll either higher or lower. Having this understanding will help you find the approaches that effectively reduce your stress, instead of inadvertently adding to it.

The Stress Reaction Cycle

It may seem like stress is an external force—something that happens to you, such as a rude driver, a work deadline, or the illness of a loved one. As a result, it may seem like there's nothing you can do about your stress, but this simply isn't the case. You may not be able to shape the world so that nothing stressful ever happens to you again, but you can change the way you respond to stress, which can make all the difference in how you feel.

The most fundamental thing to understand about stress is that it isn't a one-time event with one cause and one reaction. It's actually a cycle with many phases, which means there are multiple opportunities to interrupt it before it turns into a full-blown chain reaction. Psychologists refer to it as the stress reaction cycle, and this is what it looks like from a bird's eye view:

Chapter 2: The Role of Stress   19

YOUR BODY KNOWS HOW TO HEAL
Your Body's Reaction to Stress

Autonomic Nervous System Has Two Subsections

SYMPATHETIC & PARASYMPATHETIC

Fight or Flight Reaction

Sympathetic Nervous System

- Hypothalamus
- Pituitary
- Adrenal Glands
- Breathing Becomes Faster & Deeper
- Sweating Increases

Internalization of Stress

- High blood pressure
- Hyper arousal
- Arrhythmias
- Sleep disorders
- Chronic headaches, fatigue, back issues & anxiety
- Digestion is out of control
- Immune system is not working well

Maladaptive Coping
This relieves issues temporarily but does not address the root cause of stress

These are often self destructive:
- Substance abuse
- Increase in drinking alcohol
- Emotional numbing
- Gambling
- Working too much (workaholic)
- Not eating enough
- Over eating
- Social withdrawal
- Increase in caffeine
- Increase in cigarettes

Parasympathetic Nervous System

Triggered when we practice:
- Mindfulness
- Meditation
- Yoga
- Prayer
- Pranayama breathing/deep breathing
- Rest
- Acupuncture
- Massage

Using these can trigger a healing response in the body. This brings calmness and homeostasis to the body, mind, & spirit

Physiological Breakdown

- Physical & emotional exhaustion
- Loss of interest or drive
- Depression
- Anxiety
- Genetic predispositions
- Heart attack
- Stroke
- Cancer
- Autoimmune disease

Substance Dependecy

- Alcohol
- Drugs
- Cigarettes
- Cafeine
- Eating

Over the next few pages, we'll break down the individual steps in the pattern. Once you see how each of these occurrences contributes to your stress levels, you'll see just how many opportunities you have to make choices that bring more peace to your life. As you'll discover as you read this book, there is no one right way to take better care of your emotional, physical, and heart health. There are many options available to you, and understanding your own personal version of the cycle of stress will help you find the ones that work for you.

Step 1: External stressor

The external stressor is the triggering event: the snarky comment from your teenager, the car that almost hits you when you cross the street, the layoffs that are happening at work, or the suspicious-looking person walking toward you in the parking lot. This is actually the only part of the stress reaction cycle that your mind and body don't play a direct role in.

Step 2: Internal appraisal

Internal appraisal comes either just before, during, or after the actual trigger occurs. Your senses, such as your sight, hearing, and what's commonly known as your intuition or gut, take in the information that something's not right. Your body is exquisitely wired to scan for danger and assess safety. This ability to know when your environment is safe or unsafe is called neuroception, and it happens without you even being conscious of it.

When your senses detect something that they perceive to be a threat, they send a signal to your amygdala, which is an almond-shaped part of your brain responsible for processing emotions, particularly strong emotions such as fear and pleasure. When the amygdala is triggered, it sends a signal to the hypothalamus and the pituitary gland, two other sections of the brain responsible for maintaining homeostasis (a fancy word for "balance") in the body. They communicate with the rest of the body through the autonomic nervous system; this is the part of your nervous system that regulates the many processes that occur without your conscious awareness, such as your heart rate, blood pressure, metabolism, respiration, and sleep. Again, this is all occurring beneath the level of your awareness—just as your body knows how to heal, it also knows how to take care of you during stressful situations.

Step 3: Physiological response

After the hypothalamus and the pituitary receive the call that there's danger present, they activate the sympathetic nervous system (SNS), which is the half of the autonomic nervous system that rules the flight-or-fight response. They do this by cueing the adrenal glands, which are located right above your kidneys in your lower back and release stress hormones such as adrenaline and cortisol. The flight-or-fight response stimulates the cardiovascular system (accelerating the heart rate and diverting blood to the extremities) and the musculoskeletal (priming you to be able to get out of there or to stay and fight). Whenever the SNS is activated, it means the other half of the autonomic nervous system—the parasympathetic nervous system, which governs the rest-and-digest functions of the body—is suppressed, because they can't both be activated at the same time. As a result, your immune system and digestive systems are given the "stand down" signal and you are left in a state of hyperarousal. This physiological link between stress and digestion likely explains why a 2018 survey of more than 71,000 people found that 61 percent of Americans report having had at least one gastrointestinal symptom (such as heartburn, abdominal pain, bloating, diarrhea, and constipation) in the past week.[11]

If we don't recognize these symptoms as what they are—warning signs—we won't be inspired to take the steps to counteract them. We subconsciously perpetuate the problem.

It's really about what happens after this point that determines how much stress you're under at any given time, and how big of a response you'll have to each successive stressor. The more time you typically exist in a state of hyperarousal, the larger a physiological stress response you can have, with more adrenaline and cortisol released and a bigger impact on the major systems of the body.

Step 4: Internalization

Internalization is where your response to stress starts to become something that you are at least partially aware of. You may notice that your heart is racing, your stomach is upset, or your back is aching. And then you may start to worry about how you feel, and how well or how poorly you perceive yourself to be handling the stress. This is when you may start thinking things like, "Just calm down," "Why is this happening?" or, "Nothing ever works out for me!" These types of thoughts can lead to mental symptoms such as worry, anxiety, or dread. Any of these thought patterns are unpleasant, and a desire to not feel the emotional effects of those thoughts leads to the next step in the cycle.

We will talk much more about the psychological contributors to the stress response in Chapter 3, and dig into tools that will help alleviate them.

Step 5: Maladaptive coping

When you start to notice that you are in physical and/or emotional distress, you will choose to do something to alleviate that discomfort. What methods you choose in this moment dictate whether the stress response lessens, or whether it gets worse.

Whether you realize it or not, you have a habitual response to stress. And for the overwhelming majority of us, this habitual response isn't actually helpful. The technical term for a response that doesn't relieve the triggering problem is *maladaptive*. Nearly everyone alive on the planet engages in at least one maladaptive coping mechanism in the face of stress, and most of us have several that we turn to regularly. Meaning, it's very likely that you have at least one habitual response to stress that is not making your life any easier. In fact, the thing you're hoping will make you feel better probably only makes you feel worse—typically, much worse.

Maladaptive coping mechanisms can rely on outside substances, such as food, alcohol, cigarettes, caffeine, or pharmaceutical or recreational drugs. Or, they may be more behavioral. Perhaps you pour yourself into your job and overwork, or you distract yourself with mindless media and constantly checking your phone, or you become hyperactive and just can't seem to sit still. Or your reactions may have an emotional component and you jump to anger, worry, or feeling overwhelmed.

These mechanisms perpetuate the physiological stress response in the body so that you stay in a state of hyperarousal. This means that you will subconsciously perceive more potential stressors of greater danger because your sympathetic nervous system stays on high alert, and it takes less stimulation from the amygdala, hypothalamus, and pituitary to spring into action. In addition, all those high-calorie comfort foods, alcoholic drinks, cigarettes, and drugs have physical side effects that can push your body from homeostasis into full-on breakdown.

When I was regularly suffering from ventricular tachycardia due to the stresses of my job, my maladaptive coping mechanisms were not eating enough and over caffeinating. I would skip meals because I felt I didn't have time to grocery shop and prepare meals, and then I would drink several cups of coffee a day to give myself the energy to keep going. Although I thought I was responding to my circumstances in a beneficial way, I was actually only stimulating myself further and contributing to my racing heart rate. I also skipped exercise, which would have been a healthy outlet for that stress, as well as beneficial for my cardiovascular health. Then I drank too much alcohol on the weekends to help take my edge off, which made me sleep poorly and need more caffeine.

There's a quirk of human psychology that also works against us when it comes to managing our stress. It's what Sigmund Freud, the father of modern psychology, called the repetition compulsion, or "the desire to return to an earlier state of things." But these attempts only hurt us more by leading to rumination (thinking repeatedly about things that have already happened) and negative patterns in reactions and behaviors.

We crave familiarity and a sense of safety, which is not a negative impulse. The problem comes when we become familiar with things that actually only perpetuate our discomfort, such as the maladaptive coping mechanisms that I mentioned above. It's why it can be so hard to break a habit of a nightly glass or two (or three, or four) of wine; you are subconsciously seeking that feeling of familiarity by holding the glass in your hand, and enjoying the comforting flush of an alcoholic buzz. You want that feeling so badly, in fact, that you completely overlook the fact that drinking alcohol interrupts your sleep, makes you foggy-headed in the morning, and contributes to the extra pounds you're carrying around that are leading to aches and pains that don't resolve themselves.

Because of the repetition compulsion, your maladaptive behavior can become not just a one-time choice, but a cycle that's hard to break. I'm telling you about it not to make you feel like there's no hope of changing how you feel, but to show you that you're wired to seek relief in ways that aren't actually that helpful. I want you to give yourself a break, because beating yourself up won't help you break the cycle and make more helpful choices.

Step 6: Breakdown

When you experience stress, and then perpetuate and worsen that stress with the coping mechanisms you choose, your health becomes compromised and it is only a matter of time until you enter breakdown.

In other words, the stress itself is harmful to the body, and the ways you cope with that stress can most certainly cause further harm.

Perhaps, like I did, you skimp on sleep and then over-rely on caffeine to keep going when things get stressful. The caffeine raises your overall level of physiological stimulation and makes you more prone to stress as the lack of sleep causes your immunity to dip, so you get sick more often, which causes even more stress. Caffeine can also increase blood pressure and may damage artery walls, as can alcohol and cigarettes. So the things you're choosing to manage your stress with may be making things much worse.

Or maybe you rely on poor-quality, non-nutritious, high-calorie foods because they're easier to find and prepare, and they provide some short-term emotional comfort. But they also cause you to gain weight, perhaps to the point that you become clinically obese, which is defined as a Body Mass Index (a measure of your weight in kilograms divided by the square of your height in meters) of 30 or higher by the Center for Disease Control and Prevention.[12] Obesity is a risk factor for multiple other diseases, including heart disease, as well as osteoarthritis, and type 2 diabetes. You start to develop symptoms of these other diseases, and your quality of life drops dramatically. Perhaps the illness is even life-threatening.

The good news in all of this is that learning to interrupt your own stress reaction cycle is as good for your heart as it is for all other parts of your life.

A Deeper Look at the Chemicals of Stress

During the body's physiological response to stress—or step number 3 in the stress response cycle—I mentioned that the pituitary will cue the adrenal glands to secrete cortisol and adrenaline in an effort to prepare the body to flee or to fight. Let's take a closer look at what these hormones do to your body.

Adrenaline causes your breathing to accelerate, your heart rate to speed up, and your blood pressure to rise. While these are helpful responses in that they prepare us to deal with a threat, they are also early warning signs of heart disease. When we never get out of the stress response and allow the body to shift into a relaxed state, we set in motion the early stages of heart disease. Chronic stress then contributes to inflammation throughout the body, including in the coronary arteries, which sets the stage even further for heart disease.

High levels of cortisol from long-term stress have been linked to increased cholesterol, triglycerides (a type of fat in the blood), and blood pressure. These three results are each a risk factor for heart disease; when cortisol is released, it triggers the body to release more blood sugar to be used as fuel in case you need to run or fight. Those blood sugar levels then cause more triglycerides to form. Cortisol also promotes the buildup of plaque in the arteries that deliver blood from the heart to the rest of the body; in fact, research has found that the higher your exposure to cortisol, the more plaque you have in your coronary arteries.[13] When enough plaque builds up, the artery becomes blocked, which can result in a heart attack. High triglycerides are believed to contribute to thickening of the arterial walls, making arteries less pliable and with less room inside for blood to flow, resulting in higher blood pressure. And when blood pressure is high, it can damage the walls of your blood vessels and your heart, while also increasing the risk of a stroke.

Cortisol has also been linked to weight gain, particularly around the waist. A 2017 study measured cortisol levels in hair samples of 2,527 women and men who were fifty-four years of age and older, and found that high cortisol levels were associated with larger waists, higher body mass indices (a measure of obesity), and weighing more than those with lower cortisol levels.[14] Your waist size matters because it is a primary predictor of heart disease—if you carry more weight around your waist than your hips, your risk of developing heart disease is elevated. The risk is significantly elevated if your waist size is greater than approximately thirty-five inches.[15]

When your hypothalamus and pituitary signal the adrenals to release cortisol, they also simultaneously send the message to the thyroid to make less thyroid hormone. The thyroid regulates metabolism, growth, the menstrual cycle, muscle strength, and more—all important things, unless you are currently facing a situation that is cueing the stress response. In that case, your body wants to put all its resources toward facing the threat. And so the thyroid gets the signal to stand down. Too little thyroid hormone can then lead to a slower heart rate, a further increase in cholesterol levels, and a reduction in blood vessel function. It is very common for women to have low thyroid function, yet few doctors make the connection. If you know you have an underactive thyroid, it's even more important that you take great care of your heart.

Signs Your Thyroid May Be Out of Whack

According to the American Association of Clinical Endocrinologists, thirty million Americans have some form of thyroid disorder. Of that number, half (fifteen million) don't realize they have it. And women are ten times more likely than men to have thyroid issues.

Because your thyroid health is so tied to your heart health—not to mention that it's responsible for much of how you feel, how much you weigh, how clearly you think, and how much energy you have—you'll want to keep an eye out for the symptoms associated with a struggling thyroid gland. If you notice any of these, be sure to address it with your primary care physician or integrative health practitioner; disorders can be diagnosed with a simple blood test, and remedies range from prescription medication, to supplements, to dietary changes.

Signs of hypothyroidism (too little thyroid hormone)
- Fatigue that lingers even after you've had a good night's sleep
- Low mood, even clinical depression
- Unexplained weight gain, with extra pounds very difficult to lose
- Forgetfulness and brain fog
- Low sex drive
- Constipation
- Dry, itchy skin
- Ridged and/or flaky nails
- Changes in menstrual cycle: periods last longer, are heavier, and may occur closer together
- Unexplained muscle aches and twinges, particularly in the extremities
- Increase in blood pressure
- Feeling cold all the time
- Hair loss—on head, body, and/or at outer edges of eyebrows
- Increased levels of LDL, or "bad", cholesterol

Signs of hyperthyroidism (too much thyroid hormone)
- Anxiousness, particularly to the point that it's hard to ever relax
- Increased appetite
- Unexplained weight loss
- Difficulty concentrating
- Heart palpitations or a racing heartbeat
- Overactive bowels or diarrhea
- Changes in menstrual cycle: periods get lighter and further apart
- Increase in blood pressure
- You tend to run warm and sweat easily
- Difficulty falling asleep or waking up to racing thoughts in the middle of the night
- Thinning hair

One hormone we women have working for us when it comes to heart protection is estrogen. This reproductive hormone affects nearly every cell in the body; scientists are still discovering all the roles it plays. When it comes to heart health, what we know so far is that estrogen keeps blood vessels pliable, and they respond better to the accelerated heart rate and increase in blood pressure that follows a stressful event. It also helps to keep cholesterol at healthy levels, and it soaks up destructive free radicals that could otherwise damage heart and circulatory cells. While this is good news, the difficulty arises when we hit menopause and our estrogen production drops dramatically. As a result, our blood vessels lose that protection and our risk for heart disease goes up. The benefits of estrogen likely explain why the average age of a heart attack in women is seventy years of age, whereas in men it's only sixty-six. So if you're peri- or post-menopausal, your declining estrogen levels give you an additional risk factor for heart disease.

Other risk factors that affect women exclusively, or significantly more than men, are gestational diabetes, endometriosis, polycystic ovarian syndrome, and migraines. Endometriosis has been found to raise the risk of heart disease by 400 percent in women under forty! Birth control pills also contribute to clotting, while five or more pregnancies increases lipoproteins—the substances that transport cholesterol and triglycerides in the blood.

But the stacking of the deck against us doesn't stop there: women also have smaller hearts than men, as well as smaller interior chambers of the heart with thinner walls between the chambers. Meaning, our hearts are just not built quite as sturdily as men's are. Our hearts also function differently. When we are stressed, our pulse increases and our heart pumps more blood. When men are stressed, their arteries constrict and their blood pressure rises. For this reason, one of the primary cardiovascular disease diagnostic tests—the angiogram—tests to find narrowing or blockages in the large arteries of the heart. But women tend to develop blockages in the smaller arteries. You can go get an angiogram and be given the thumbs-up by your doctor, but still be at risk for heart attack. (If that happens and you continue to experience any of the symptoms listed on pages 31–32, do not pass go and do not collect $200—go immediately to see a doctor who specializes in women's heart disease.)

I may sound alarmist, but the truth is, traditional medicine does not have a good track record at identifying and treating heart disease in women. A woman who has a heart attack generally stays in the hospital longer, and is more likely to die before leaving the hospital than a man. They are also more likely to develop a blood clot that can lead to a second heart attack, yet they are less likely to be given anticlotting medication. Disturbingly, women are also more likely than men to have a second heart attack within a year of the first.

Perhaps most frustratingly, many doctors simply aren't familiar with the symptoms that frequently precede a heart attack. If you go to the emergency room complaining of pressure in your upper abdomen, fatigue, and a cold sweat (all symptoms more typical in women than in men, see the sidebar on pages 31–32 for more), you are likely to be told it's something you ate and be sent home, whereas a man complaining of chest pain will be treated swiftly for possible heart attack. If you're thinking that you can rely on your doctor to keep your heart healthy, I'm so sorry to say, you're more than likely wrong.

Symptoms of Heart Attack in Women

We've all seen a movie where a man has experienced a heart attack. He clutches his chest, winces in pain, and then falls to the floor. While this image has been burned into our collective unconscious, it doesn't reflect the reality of how women experience a heart attack. Our symptoms are much different and much less known.

When Rosie O'Donnell had a heart attack in 2012, she helped spread awareness of just how differently the sexes experience heart attacks when she shared what she experienced: nausea, a cold sweat that made her feel clammy, and an ache in her arms and chest. Like many women who have heart attacks, she didn't know what was happening. And it's no wonder—those symptoms could point to any number of less serious illnesses, particularly the flu.

To help you identify whether the physical sensation you're experiencing might be heart related, here are the most common heart attack symptoms women experience:

- **Upper body pain or pressure.** The heart itself doesn't have many nerve endings, so the pain may travel to locations that do, including the arms (particularly the left arm), shoulder blades, back, neck, jaw, and even the teeth. It may also show up as numbness, tingling, and ache, or a sensation of pressure rather than outright pain. Typically, however, the sensation doesn't travel below the belly button.
- **Chest pain that comes and goes.** You may feel a squeezing sensation in the middle of your chest, or it may feel like uncomfortable pressure or even pain. (It may feel like heartburn.) This sensation may go away and then come back, or it may persist for more than a few minutes.
- **Difficulty catching your breath.** Women are more likely to have shortness of breath during a heart attack than men. In fact, 42 percent of women report feeling short of breath just before having a heart attack, and nearly 58 percent experience it during the attack itself.[16] When it occurs as a warning sign of an impending heart attack, windedness seems to happen with very little exertion and stops when you rest. During the attack itself, it is often the first symptom and it continues or worsens as the attack progresses.
- **Fatigue.** This isn't your garden variety didn't-get-enough-sleep feeling. In the days or weeks leading up to an attack, because your heart is struggling to deliver oxygen to your body, you wake up feeling tired and struggle to get your normal amount of tasks completed with no cause that you can pinpoint. You may also have trouble sleeping, or a sudden change in sleep habits. The feeling only gets worse until you are completely wiped out and feel too tired to do anything.
- **Cold sweat.** That clammy feeling could be a flu symptom, but it could also be a sign that your heart is in distress—particularly when combined with any of the other symptoms listed here.

- **Stomach upset.** Women are twice as likely to have stomach-related symptoms than men during a heart attack, whether that feels like nausea or indigestion, or includes actual vomiting.
- **Light-headedness.** You may experience dizziness or even fainting, perhaps caused by low blood pressure due to poorly functioning heart valves or partially blocked arteries that reduce blood flow.
- **Sudden rise in anxiety.** Your mood can also be an indicator that your heart is under duress; anxiety that comes on rapidly for no apparent reason, some even call it a sense of impending doom, particularly when coupled with a cold sweat, shortness of breath, and/or unexplained pain or pressure anywhere from the belly button up is a reason to call 911.

What to do During a Heart Attack

If you find yourself experiencing one or more of these indicators, the best thing to do is to call 911. Don't wait to feel better! And don't drive yourself to the hospital unless you truly have no other choice. Once you've called for assistance, then take slow, deep breaths to stay calm as possible. Help is on the way.

Exercise: Take a Look at Your Responses to Stress

You may immediately know some of the things you do to help you cope with stress, but others you may not be fully aware of. To start to see how you might be choosing maladaptive coping mechanisms, take a moment to write down all the things you do when you are stressed.

- What do you do in the moment when you're feeling stressed?
- What do you do at the end of a stressful day to help you wind down?
- What do you do to help you gear up for a busy day when you're already feeling like you're at max capacity?

Write it all down. Later in the book, we will start to replace these maladaptive coping mechanisms with practices that actually help trigger the relaxation response and provide a true antidote to stress, but the first step is to allow yourself to see what you're already doing, and how you have likely been contributing to your own stress levels.

The Way out of a Chronic Stress Response

Just as your body has physiological mechanisms that help you respond to stressors, it has an equally powerful system that helps you relax. This is ruled by the parasympathetic nervous system, which, as I mentioned earlier in this chapter, governs your rest and digest functions.

If the sympathetic nervous system steps on the gas pedal of your heart, the parasympathetic nervous system applies the brakes.

If your parasympathetic nervous system isn't well toned, your heartbeat will be erratic, and what's known as your heart rate variability, will suffer, which is a predictor of heart disease.

Spending more time in the parasympathetic realm—something you'll learn exactly how to do in Section 2 of this book—also cues deeper emotions, such as compassion, in what's known as the tend-and-befriend response. This drive to connect with others is really what motivates you to wander into the office kitchen during a hectic day. You're looking for someone to talk to, even though you may think you're there to see if there are any leftover pastries from the morning breakfast meeting. When you spend more time in the parasympathetic realm, you not only benefit your physical health, you tend to your emotional health because it sets the stage for you to deepen your relationships, develop a support network, and exercise your compassion. This helps you find the support you need to start making changes in how you deal with your stressors.

Before we get into the tools that will help reduce the stress in your life and in your body, you need to understand how your thoughts, feelings, and mood also contribute to or detract from heart health. Your heart is much more than just a muscle—it's also the seat of your emotions. In the next chapter, we'll unpack how to take care of your emotional heart so that your physical heart stays as healthy as it can be.

CHAPTER 3

THE PSYCHOLOGY OF HEART DISEASE

In addition to an extremely high stress level, the patients I see have something else in common. They think there's something wrong with them because they can't seem to find their way out of the strong emotions—such as anger, anxiety, or depression—that they are experiencing. Worse yet, it makes them feel that they are somehow unequipped to deal with their lives.

The first thing I do with anyone who comes to see me is to get them to see how a chronically elevated stress level is a very natural reaction to our modern lives. After we take an objective look at all the stressors they are facing at one time, I can see the relief wash over them, they're not weak or failing at life. They're legitimately dealing with a lot, and nearly anyone in their same situation would be feeling the same level of stress.

The second thing I do is help them unpack the emotions they're feeling as a result of their stressors. Of course, I address their emotional health because I'm a holistic mental health counselor and that is my specialty. But I also know that when you learn how to work with your emotions more skillfully, everything benefits. Your physical health—and particularly your heart health—improves. Your belief in yourself rises. And you find it easier to connect with others and get the support you need to face your stressors with strength, confidence, and trust.

The Power of Emotions to Hurt or to Heal the Body

The truth is, your emotional response to stress may be a greater risk factor for heart problems than smoking, high blood pressure, and high cholesterol. As an example, research has shown that if stress makes you very angry or anxious, you're more likely to have heart disease or a heart attack.[17]

That's because every emotion you feel has a physiological effect on the cells of your body, especially the cells of the heart, which is the command center of the body. After all, it is responsible for pumping blood and delivering important nutrients to every other part of your body. Your heart is vital for homeostasis. If your heart is heavy because you are carrying pain, disappointment, sadness, trauma, guilt, and/or shame, it can affect every organ in your body.

As a yoga teacher with a PhD in metaphysics, I have learned that the energy of the heart is all about self-love and self-care first, and love for others second. When you have love for yourself, then your heart's energy is able to extend to others, including family, friends, your community, and the world at large. That means your heart needs self-love and self-care to thrive. So many of us women get this backward—we think that we'll take care of ourselves after we've taken care of everyone else around us. We rarely show ourselves enough love and do the things that make us feel cared for, because we're simply too busy caring for others. It's a theme I see in at least 80 percent of my clients. But there is one client whose story is a perfect example of how we take on what feels like too much, and worse, how we often feel like we have no choice.

Jessica is in her mid-thirties (as with all the names of clients I share in this book, Jessica's has been changed to protect her privacy). She works as an ER nurse. It's a stressful job, but it pays well. Jessica is single and doesn't have children. She also lost her mother several years ago. When she did, the responsibility of taking care of a ninety-six-year-old grandmother fell on Jessica's shoulders, despite the fact that she has a brother who is perfectly capable of sharing the load. They come from a culture where caretaking responsibilities almost always fall to the daughter.

Jessica supports her grandmother financially, and she can only afford to pay for so much caretaking help. (Jessica's parents are divorced and her father isn't that involved in family life.) So in addition to her job and taking care of herself, Jessica is also cleaning, cooking, buying groceries, and scheduling and attending doctors' appointments with her grandmother. Jessica loves her grandmother, but she also feels lonely with no one to share her burdens. She's grieving the loss of her mother, and she is angry at her brother for neglecting his responsibilities. Jessica tries to get her brother to help. He's supposed to go check in on the grandmother on Tuesdays, Wednesdays, and Thursdays—the nights when Jessica has to work late—but he often blows it off. Or if he does go, he doesn't do the things he's supposed to do, like give the grandmother her medications. When Jessica realizes what's happened, she'll yell at her brother or send him an angry text, which only devolves into a texting war.

Because she's so busy and stressed, Jessica is eating a lot of processed comfort foods—anything she can pick up quickly. It's caused her to gain weight, which she doesn't feel great about. She's starting to display symptoms of anxiety and depression, and who can blame her? The fact that she's feeling tense and at times helpless makes sense—anyone in a similar situation would likely feel the same way.

I see so many clients come into my office who are in a similar spot. They are doing so much and feeling taken advantage of and unappreciated by their families. They're struggling with anger, and then shame and guilt at being angry at their family members. It's an emotional stew that weighs heavily on the heart.

The Molecules of Emotion

You are probably aware that the emotions you feel have an effect on your body. When you're sad, you cry; when you're nervous, you sweat; and when you're mad, your face turns red. But there is a much deeper connection between the emotions you feel and your physiological reality. This is what people are referring to when they talk about the mind-body connection; what we think affects how we feel, and how we feel affects our body.

Much of what we know scientifically about the mind-body connection is thanks to the work of Candace Pert, a molecular biologist who is widely considered the mother of the field of study known as psychoneuroimmunology—a branch of science that studies the connection between the brain and the immune system.

Pert's book, *Molecules of Emotion*, is one of my all-time favorites. She explains how every emotion we feel causes the brain to release a specific chemical that is then delivered to cells throughout the body where they initiate a specific response. For example, when you're embarrassed, the brain releases peptides that cause your cheeks to flush. However, emotions do more than just cause surface physiological changes. They can also trigger the stress response, which then affects the immune system. In other words, the things you feel affect your health, particularly your heart health. Or as Pert puts it: "The body is the unconscious mind!"

The power emotions have to influence your health works both ways. Just as negative emotions can have negative effects on immunity and health, positive emotions can release chemicals that influence the immune system positively—mobilizing fighter cells to destroy a tumor, for example. Pert was instrumental in showing how techniques such as meditation and visualization (which you'll learn in Chapter 7) can help create those positive emotional states.

Ironically, Pert's own life was a perfect example of how living in this world without taking great care of yourself can have a negative impact on your heart. Pert was an instrumental part of the research team that discovered the receptor in the brain that opioids fit into—like a key into a lock—as a graduate student at Johns Hopkins University School of Medicine in the 1970s. Actually, Pert carried on with her experiments despite the fact that her professor had told her to stop doing them. Then in 1978, her professor was awarded the prestigious Lasker Award (considered a precursor for the Nobel Prize) for the discovery, and she was not mentioned at all. Pert spoke up about this injustice, writing to the foundation that issued the award and saying that she had "played a key role in initiating the research and following it up." She wrote that she was "angry and upset to be excluded." She was basically shunned by the scientific community for advocating for herself and her work.

Pert was a woman in a field dominated by men, and the discrimination she endured as a result took a toll on her—how could it not? Having your voice discounted or silenced absolutely impacts your heart. It causes you to start doubting yourself, and can lead to feelings of worthlessness and anger. As a woman, you may not realize just how big of a mental burden it can be to be part of a long history and system that views women as less than men. That mental burden affects your heart and can lead to cardiovascular disease, but it is an undeniable reality.

Pert was very candid about how she struggled to take care of herself by eating well, exercising, and meditating, and as a result she didn't really find homeostasis in her life. She ended up dying of cardiac arrest at age sixty-seven.

This is why it's so important that you have picked up this book. You can learn how to work with your emotions so that you don't have to stay stuck in old emotional patterns that can degrade your health and wear on your heart over time. That's why I want to talk about the emotions I see most commonly in my practice, so that you can begin to identify if you are prone to them, and learn what to do about them if you are.

Anxiety

Mentally, anxiety tends to become present as hypervigilance, accompanied by racing thoughts that tend to incorporate worry and fear. It can even be so overwhelming that it brings on feelings of impending doom. Physiologically, anxiety is often accompanied by heart palpitations, nausea, and sweaty or trembling palms. If you tend toward anxiety, your body reacts in ways that can put an extra strain on your heart. This includes a racing heartbeat, increased blood pressure, and a sense of being on high alert. Anxiety keeps your sympathetic nervous system in a heightened state, which tends to keep your heart beating faster and your blood pressure higher.

Anxiety may have an association with the following heart disorders and cardiac risk factors:

- **Rapid heart rate (tachycardia):** In serious cases, a rapid heart rate can interfere with normal heart function and increase the risk of sudden cardiac arrest.
- **Increased blood pressure:** If chronic, high blood pressure can lead to coronary disease, weakening of the heart muscle, and heart failure.
- **Decreased heart rate variability:** This variability in heart rate may result in higher incidence of death after an acute heart attack.

Anxiety and depression are two different things, although anxiety can lead to depression.

Symptoms of anxiety

- Agitation
- Social isolation
- Anger
- Irritability
- Increase in appetite
- Restlessness
- Fatigue
- Inability to concentrate
- Hypervigilance
- Racing thoughts
- Worry
- Fear
- Feelings of impending doom
- Heart palpitations
- Trembling or sweaty palms
- Nausea

Loneliness

The other common psychological state I see in a majority of my clients is a feeling of loneliness. This pervasive feeling of being all alone is present in so many women, whether or not they are married or have children. Many of them have had these feelings even since childhood.

Humans are social creatures; we evolved living in tribes. Feeling disconnected from others can cause a low-grade yet continuous level of stress that takes its toll on our heart health and mental health. And with so many of us moving often and living away from family and friends, isolation is more common than ever.

Loneliness is also often a reflection of feeling disconnected from a higher power, which can make you feel truly alone in this world.

One of my clients, Sara, has two adorable preschool-aged children. Her husband is in the military and just moved to Massachusetts from Louisiana. Even though she has a family of her own, she feels trapped inside her house with her two kids and no fellow grown-ups to talk to because her husband is deployed. Most of us don't live in a neighborhood where there is a group of women on our street talking over each other's fences anymore. Everyone's working and must tend to their own schedules of work and family obligations. The pace of our lives makes it harder to connect. Getting together takes effort to make a plan, and then still follow through during the inevitable last-minute conflicts and rescheduling that happens. Honestly, even in my own life when I finally make a date to meet up with friends, they're either distracted by their children or their phones, and the conversation isn't very deep.

It's also hard to find healthy people to hang around with. Another of my clients, Linda, had a big sales executive job with a very good salary before she got laid off. Luckily, she received a good severance package and has already found another job, but the time off from work helped her realize the estrangement she was feeling from the friends she's had since junior high school—she'd never had the time to notice how unhealthy those relationships were. Her husband also recently had an affair, and when she comes into my office, she talks about how alone she feels. "I don't have anybody I can connect to as a friend who is a healthy person I can trust and confide in," she tells me. Linda is lucky to have a close relationship with her sister, but she doesn't want to overburden this important relationship. She also wants a best friend. The problem is, after the betrayal of her husband, Linda really doesn't trust anyone. And if you're not trusting, how will you connect to someone? So many of the women I know and counsel can relate.

The surest way to counteract those feelings of isolation is to find time to quiet the mind through meditation or a body scan (both of which we'll cover in Chapter 7). When you do, you gain access to an inner wisdom that can make you feel more guided and cared for, both of which make you feel less lonely. As you learn to trust that energy, you will invariably find that it will help guide you to the right people who will bring healthy relationships into your life.

Feelings of isolation can lead to depression—a feeling of wanting to stay in bed with the shades down, because it feels safer than trying to connect with people who may ultimately only let you down. As tempting as it may sound, isolating yourself only fosters that heavy-hearted feeling. If you don't want to leave the house, at least meditate! It will help you find the open-heartedness and the confidence to seek out fulfilling relationships again.

Depression

Depression is a common condition that negatively impacts how you feel mentally, emotionally, and physically. Mentally, it can cause you to lose interest in things you once enjoyed doing; emotionally, it often creates feelings of sadness or apathy; physically, it can make even the simplest things, like getting out of bed, feel difficult.

The American Psychiatry Association estimates that one in six people will become depressed at some point in their life, and that women are more likely to experience depression than men.[18] Research has found that women who suffer from depression have an 18 percent higher risk of having a heart attack and a 44 percent higher likelihood of having a stroke than women who don't.[19] And women are nearly twice as likely as men to suffer from depression in the first place.[20]

Part of the reason the two conditions are so linked is that when you are depressed, it's hard to do the things you need to do to take care of yourself, like exercise and eating a healthy diet. But depression also causes physical changes that are conducive to cardiovascular disease:

- **Low-grade inflammation**, which can contribute to both the accumulation of plaque within the arteries and hardening of the arterial walls so that they become less pliable.
- **Production of stress hormones increases**, which, as we learned in the previous chapters, also play a role in heart disease.
- **Platelets—or blood cell fragments—are more likely to clump** together and form clots in the bloodstream that can lead to stroke.
- **Cholesterol levels**—research has found that women with depression have reduced levels of the "good," or high-density lipoprotein (HDL), cholesterol. Depression can also foster or exacerbate a sense of isolation.

A Harvard study[21] found that women who had either been diagnosed with depression or were taking an anti-depressant had an over 40 percent greater likelihood of having a stroke compared to women who hadn't been diagnosed with depression or taken an anti-depressant.

Pennsylvania researchers[22] also did a study where they asked women the following three questions:

- Do you often feel sad or depressed?
- Do you often feel helpless?
- Do you often feel downhearted and blue?

They found that women who answered "yes" to any of those questions were more than twice as likely to develop heart disease within five years than women who answered no to all three questions. Women who reported feeling helpless had the greatest risk.

> ### Symptoms of depression
>
> - Feeling tearful or crying nearly every day
> - Markedly diminished interest in activities you used to enjoy
> - Significant weight loss or weight gain; increase or decrease in appetite
> - Difficulty getting to sleep, staying asleep, or sleeping too much nearly every day
> - Restlessness, pacing, or picking at clothes, or talking very quietly with slow speech
> - Fatigue, tiredness, or loss of energy nearly every day
> - Feelings of worthlessness or guilt every day
> - Inability to think clearly, easily distracted
> - Recurrent thoughts of death

From an energetic perspective, depression is the result of assuming too much burden; as a result, you don't feel you have the time and energy to do the self-love and self-care you need for optimal wellness and heart health.

A powerful way to relieve the burden on your heart is through forgiveness. And the first person you need to forgive is yourself. After all, you're not superhuman. You can't possibly take on everything that your family and the world will try to impose on you. You've got to forgive yourself for not being able to do everything for everyone else. You're simply not wired that way—your heart, your command center, requires self-love and self-care *first*. That's what empowers you to do things for others. That's why you're not meant to do everything for everybody else—it's impossible! A healthy and happy you is the best way to be of service to others. Not only will it make you stronger and capable of having more impact, but seeing you take care of yourself will inspire the people around you to do it for themselves, too. And then they won't require so much of your time and energy.

In addition to being a doctor, I am also a yoga teacher, and I teach two classes a week. We always end with a body scan (a powerfully relaxing technique that you'll learn in Chapter 7) where we systematically bring our attention to each part of the body. When we're at the heart, I always point out we have to let go of the pain, upset, disappointment, sadness, and anger that might be hiding there, and send ourselves love and forgiveness to take its place.

You're not perfect, and you're not going to get everything right all the time. And you're only one person. Giving yourself a break helps your heart feel lighter, which helps you feel happier, and that absolutely shows up in your physical health.

I know that depression can be an insidious condition that clouds your thinking, but I want you to know that you aren't helpless! There are so many factors within your control—even if you are struggling with depression—that can help you feel better, bit by bit, until you are back to your normal self and your heart feels light again.

Reason #1 Why It Can Feel So Hard to Change an Emotional Response: The Repetition Compulsion

Remember, the repetition compulsion makes you yearn for a feeling of familiarity. While it can trigger you to repeat a past behavior, even one that is maladaptive, it can also reinforce habitual emotional responses. If you have a tendency toward a particular emotional reaction, whether it's anger or sadness or irritation, you will subconsciously be drawn to that emotional state simply because it is familiar to you. The good news here is that once you recognize that you're slipping back into a habitual emotion, it can inspire you to choose a coping mechanism that helps you feel better.

Reason #2 Why It Can Feel So Hard to Change an Emotional Response: Your Inherited Patterns

Whether you realize it or not, you were born into a family with its own unique patterns of maladaptive coping mechanisms, thought patterns, and beliefs. Just as you inherit eye color, height, and talent from your parents, grandparents, and great-grandparents, you can also inherit a quick temper, a tendency to put other people's needs above your own, a difficulty with setting boundaries, or a habit of reaching for alcohol or food to numb unpleasant emotions. Realizing that it's an inherited pattern can help you forgive yourself for how you've dealt with your stress in the past, and hopefully motivate you to change so that you don't keep passing the pattern on through the family tree.

My patients find it incredibly validating to learn that in their attempts to deal with the stresses that life has thrown their way, they have been repeating patterns that have been passed down through their family tree. I hope you will, too.

Recognizing what those patterns are and how they have shown up in your own choices is such a relief. It's empowering to know the truth so that you don't have to blame yourself and feel shame for obstacles you inherited.

I had a friend who felt poorly all the time. She had debilitating headaches and terrible stomachaches, yet doctors couldn't find anything wrong with her. After several months of feeling miserable and seeking relief that never came, my friend became depressed. Eventually she found a health care provider who diagnosed her with celiac disease. Although it wasn't good news, necessarily, it made her feel so much better to know there was a reason why her physical and mental health were suffering. This particular friend did not know her biological father growing up. Years later she found him and learned that he had been suffering from similar physical and mental health symptoms his entire life. She realized he had also been suffering from celiac disease. It was undiagnosed his entire life. Recognizing what issues you may have been born with helps you not feel crazy.

My favorite tool for identifying your personal inherited patterns is called a genogram. It looks like a typical family tree, except it records a lot more information than dates of birth and death. A genogram captures emotional, behavioral, and genetic information that can help you make more sense of your challenges and help you make better choices in how you respond to them.

To create your own genogram, start by drawing a small square to represent yourself down toward the bottom right-hand corner of a piece of paper. Use solid lines to connect that square to other squares on the same horizontal line that represent your siblings. Just above your square, draw two squares to represent your parents and connect those two squares to the symbols you drew for you and your siblings. Then record your parents' siblings on the same horizontal line as your parents' squares. Next, record your grandparents and their siblings at the top of the page. Now you've got the skeleton of your genogram.

Now go to each square and write down the name and sex of each person. Next is the most important part—jot down any major diseases (in their physical or mental health) and personality traits that those folks have or had. Did they have a problem with alcohol or drugs? Were they depressed, anxious, or have any symptoms of mental illness? Were they known for having dramatic relationships? Or for repressing their emotions? Or for being a hothead? Record what you know about them and ask family members for their insights, too.

When you have all the information recorded, what themes can you see? Is there something you have encountered in your own life that you see mirrored in your genogram? Remember, the goal is to simply raise awareness. You may find you have a little grieving over a particular

48 *Your Body Knows How to Heal*

FAMILY GENOGRAM

Example on how to gather physical and mental illness as well as hereditary and psychological patterns in your family

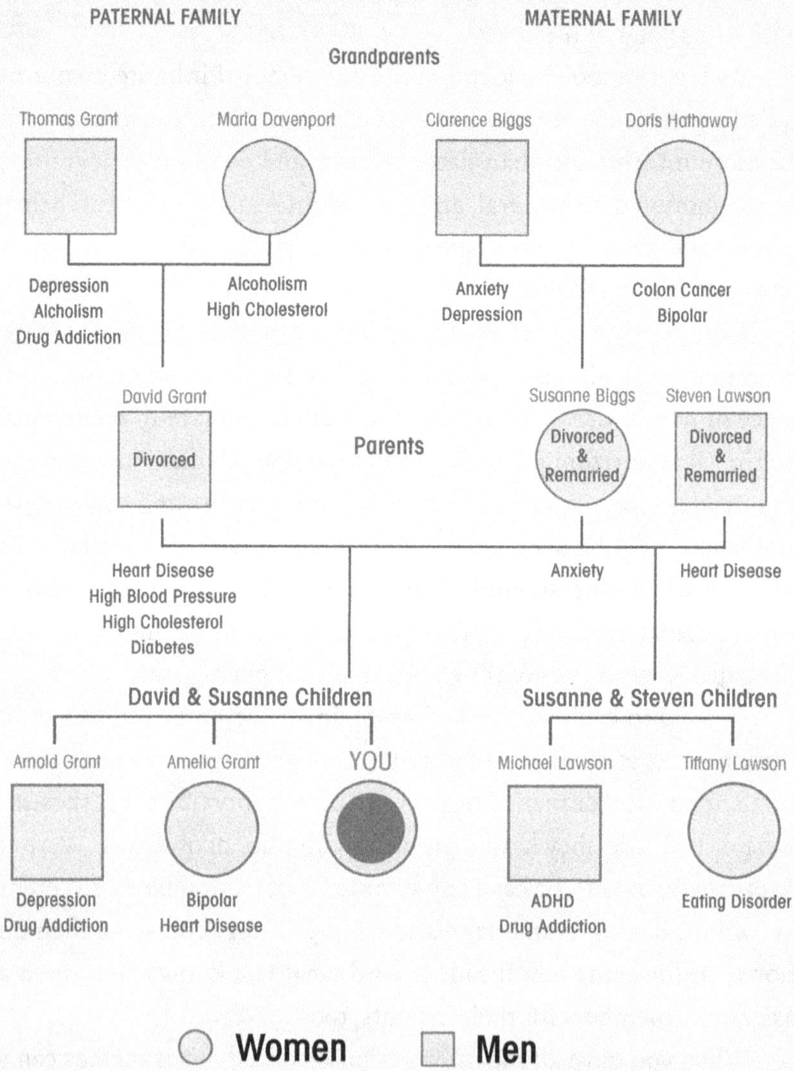

PATERNAL FAMILY   **MATERNAL FAMILY**

Grandparents

Thomas Grant	Maria Davenport	Clarence Biggs	Doris Hathaway
Depression Alcholism Drug Addiction	Alcoholism High Cholesterol	Anxiety Depression	Colon Cancer Bipolar

Parents

David Grant		Susanne Biggs	Steven Lawson
Divorced		Divorced & Remarried	Divorced & Remarried
Heart Disease High Blood Pressure High Cholesterol Diabetes		Anxiety	Heart Disease

David & Susanne Children   Susanne & Steven Children

Arnold Grant	Amelia Grant	YOU	Michael Lawson	Tiffany Lawson
Depression Drug Addiction	Bipolar Heart Disease		ADHD Drug Addiction	Eating Disorder

◯  **Women**   ▢  **Men**

challenge that your family members have faced, but you don't want to look at this chart and feel like nothing can be done about whatever issue you're facing. Whatever you discover, you can learn more skillful ways to handle it; you can overcome it.

A good resource for learning more about genograms is the website genopro.com. They go into more detail than I typically record when I use genograms with my clients; you don't have to do a lot of digging for these patterns to start to come into view, so don't worry too much about detail and complexity.

Choosing Better Coping Mechanisms

After you recognize your patterns, it is absolutely possible for you to break them and choose new coping mechanisms that actually support you instead of contributing to your breakdown. Just as your body has physiological mechanisms that help you respond to stressors, it has an equally powerful system that helps you relax. This is ruled by the parasympathetic nervous system, which as I mentioned earlier in this chapter, governs your "rest and digest" functions and your natural impulse to "tend and befriend" during stressful situations.

In the following two sections of this book, you'll learn many powerful tools that soothe the sympathetic nervous system and activate the parasympathetic nervous system. We'll cover practices that help both your body with diet and exercise guidelines, as well as mind-body practices including yoga, breathing exercises, conscious relaxation, mindfulness, meditation, visualizations, and affirmations. And we'll learn how to pull it all together by nurturing our spirit and letting it lead the way as we develop a personalized system of practices that is hand-tailored to meet your needs for stress relief, health, and healing.

In Jessica's case—my client who is taking care of her grandmother—a three-pronged approach has helped her feel less angry and more at peace with her situation and family dynamics. She's begun practicing two of the mindfulness techniques that she really enjoys, meditation and body scans. She's also learned to work to develop compassion for herself, her grandmother, and even her brother by learning and practicing loving-kindness meditation. She's started journaling as a way to vent every night to get it all out—something she'd never done before. It's all helping her show herself the love she's been missing since her mom died, which improves her ability to manage the responsibility of taking care of her grandmother.

Now let's start formulating a similar plan to help you make the same kind of changes.

CHAPTER 4

EATING FOR HEART HEALTH

It's impossible to have a discussion on how to improve your heart health without talking about the food you eat. Food can be either a source of support, or a source of stress to the body. Feed your body whole, nutritious, non-aggravating foods, and your body will have the building blocks it needs to run well and to heal itself from any physiological challenges you may be facing. Feed it substances (I hesitate to call them 'foods') that have been genetically modified, chemically treated, loaded with unhealthy fats, salt, and/or sugars, and 'fortified' with synthetic versions of natural nutrients, and you will be depriving yourself of those building blocks. I hope this chapter will help you start to look at your food differently, and make choices to consume things that truly feed you and support you instead of making your life harder.

There's More to Food Than Calories

Food is a source of energy—and I'm not just talking about calories. There is lifeforce in the food you eat that comes from the soil, sun, and rain. When you eat food that is still recognizable in its original form—fruits, vegetables, grains, and meat from animals that were fed their natural diet and raised in their natural habitat—you're putting that vital energy into your body.

Think about a carrot; it is a living thing. It has all the nutrients in it that it absorbed from the earth and the sun. The life energy in the carrot feeds the lifeforce in you. It makes you feel good. And when you feel good, your mind works better. You're less anxious, depressed, stressed, or angry. You don't feel bad about yourself for making a poor food choice that leaves you feeling thirsty, tired, or sick to your stomach.

When it comes to heart health, you want to support yourself on a deeper level, and that includes giving your body the nutrients and the life energy it needs to be whole. I know how busy life is today; how even getting to the grocery store, much less cooking and then cleaning up after a meal, can feel like too much. But the truth is, if you're eating junk food, you're filling yourself up with things that can cause your body a lot of harm. Processed food leads to inflammation. It also disrupts the balance between good and bad bacteria in your gut, which then contributes to anxiety and depression. These substitute foods take so much energy to digest, and yet provide so few nutrients the body can use for energy that you feel tired all the time, which affects your mood and makes it feel like too much effort to get up and take a walk or do any kind of a workout.

It's my hope that this chapter will help you look at food from a broader perspective—not just what package looks good or what marketing claim you're going to believe, but what will actually feed and nourish you instead of merely fill you up.

Although I'm not a nutritionist or a dietitian, I have made a point to study nutrition from a holistic perspective and how it contributes to mental and physical health. I've continually refined my own diet to support my health, and have advised hundreds of clients on how to do the same. I've distilled all this learning into nine pillars that form the foundation of eating for heart health.

Pillar Number One: Avoid Inflammatory Foods

Something I am continually discussing with my clients is the Empirical Dietary Inflammatory Index (EDII), a tool created by researchers from the Harvard T.H. Chan School of Public Health, Brigham and Women's Hospital, Harvard Medical School, Dana-Farber Cancer Institute, and

Massachusetts General Hospital. The EDII separates foods into two categories—inflammatory or anti-inflammatory.

Inflammatory foods provoke an immune response from the body because the body perceives them as foreign invaders and sends immune cells to attack the food, a process that creates heat, redness, and swelling that can damage your tissues. In many circumstances, such as when you accidentally cut yourself, acquire a germ that is making you sick, or you trip and twist your ankle, this inflammatory response is a natural and needed part of healing. After the tissues are repaired or germs are killed, the immune system stands down and the inflammation dissipates. But when you are continually eating foods, day after day, that your body doesn't recognize as food, this inflammation becomes chronic and can lead to the buildup of plaque in your arteries over time. This plaque impedes blood flow in the short term and can, over the long term, break off in a large chunk and form a clot that leads to heart attack or stroke.

While you can't or wouldn't even want to permanently do away with inflammation, you do want to make sure it doesn't become chronic. And the best way to do that is to remove foods that are known to cause inflammatory responses in most people. The EDII makes it easy to do so.

According to the EDII, the foods that lead to inflammation are:

- Red meat, including beef and pork, and processed meats, such as hot dogs and cold cuts
- French fries and potato chips
- Refined carbohydrates, including bread, pasta, cookies, pastries, crackers, pretzels, and bagels
- Soybean oil, corn oil, safflower oil, and canola oil
- Sugary treats, such as cakes, cookies, candy, and ice cream
- Soda
- Margarine, shortening, and lard

And foods that cool inflammation include:

- Dark, leafy vegetables, such as kale and spinach
- Darkly colored fruits, such as blueberries, blackberries, red grapes, and cherries
- Cruciferous vegetables, such as broccoli, cauliflower, cabbage, and Brussels sprouts
- Beans and lentils
- Healthy fats, such as olives, avocados, coconut oil, and olive oil
- Nuts, such as almonds, walnuts, and pistachios
- Coldwater fish, such as salmon and sardines
- Dark chocolate
- Herbs and spices
- Green tea and red wine (in moderation—meaning, no more than a glass per day for women and two glasses per day for men)

As you can see from looking at these two lists, the foods that are more natural—fruits, nuts, and beans—don't contribute to inflammation. In comparison, the foods that come in packages and have been highly processed, like cookies, pasta, and crackers, are inflammatory.

Removing inflammatory foods from your diet is one of the quickest ways to start to feel better. And when you notice that the new food choices you're making are actually helping you feel better, you'll have the motivation and the energy you need to continue on the journey to find an eating style that works for the *whole* you.

Pillar Number Two: Upgrade Your Fats

I know that fat has been demonized in our country, but it is an essential part of your diet because it plays numerous vital roles in your health. Many vitamins and minerals need fat in order to be absorbed. Fat makes up the membranes—or borders—of your cells and the coatings that surround your nerves. And it contributes to healthy muscle movement, blood clotting, and inflammation.

The problem is that there are several different kinds of fats, and some are healthier than others. So while you don't want to totally cut fat out of your diet, the way the low-fat craze suggested, you do want to be sure you're eating the kinds of fats that keep your cells, your nerves, and your heart healthy.

For the most part, that means primarily eating fats that are found in plants, such as olive oil, avocados, sunflower oil, and canola oil. Then reducing those that come from animals, like high-fat dairy, red meat, bacon, and lard.

A lot of heart health websites will tell you to eat more soybean oil, corn oil, and canola oil, but I don't recommend them as those crops are likely to be genetically modified and loaded with pesticides. Whatever oil you choose, I recommend that you spend the extra money on buying organic versions, as they cannot be genetically modified or exposed to chemical pesticides. I know it's more of an investment, but you—and your health—are worth it!

In general, the fats that come from plants are either monounsaturated or polyunsaturated, meaning they have at least one carbon atom in their chemical structure that is not bound to a hydrogen atom. Saturated fats are called that because all of the available carbon atoms are filled, or "saturated," with hydrogen atoms.

Switching to more monounsaturated and polyunsaturated fats and eating fewer saturated fats will help keep your overall LDL (the "bad" kind) cholesterol levels down. The primary reason the Mediterranean Diet is hailed as being healthy is that it is high in monounsaturated fats—primarily olive oil and olives—and low in the saturated fats that are found in red meat.

The worst kinds of fat you can eat are trans fats, which are vegetable oils that have been chemically modified so they don't become rancid and are more shelf-stable. In fact, trans fats are so dangerous to your health that they have been banned in the United States. Ironically, trans fats are also exactly what we were told to eat for many years instead of saturated fats. We were advised to replace butter with margarine, and margarine is a trans fat!

I'm not saying that saturated fats are the enemy. For every study you find that says that saturated fat contributes to heart disease, you find another that disputes this claim. Believe me, I occasionally love to enjoy some Brie cheese with whole-grain crackers as a snack. I'm only saying that it's better to keep these fats to things you eat once in a while, and not at every meal. I also talk more about eating less meat in pillar number three. I promise I'm not trying to turn you into a vegetarian! I just want to help you eat more of the things that promote health, and less of the things that don't.

Eating less saturated fat is especially good for you when you replace those calories with vegetables, nuts, and seeds—highly nutritious foods that pretty much everyone could stand to eat more of. Just promise me you won't replace those calories with highly processed foods! I hope the list below will help you pinpoint the foods to eat more of.

<u>Sources of healthy fats</u>
Olives and olive oil
Coconut oil
Grass-fed butter and ghee (clarified butter)
Avocados and avocado oil
Nuts
Wild salmon

<u>Sources of unhealthy fats</u>
Red meat, including beef, pork, bacon, and lard
Dairy, including milk, yogurt, and cheese
Trans fats, including any oil that says it is "hydrogenated" or "partially hydrogenated," and margarine

Pillar Number Three: Cut Down on Meat (and Upgrade the Meat You Do Eat)

There are a few ways that meat is troublesome from a health perspective. First, red meat (beef and pork) are sources of saturated fat, which we want to eat less of. Beyond that, the vast majority of meat available to us at grocery stores and restaurants comes from animals who are fed diets that are not natural to them. For example, cows are natural grass eaters, but are fed lots of corn. Most corn is genetically modified, and thus heavily sprayed with toxic pesticides. Since they have been genetically modified to be resilient to pesticides, farmers douse their fields with chemicals that will kill the weeds, but not the corn. The fact that the cows' digestive systems aren't able to properly digest the corn, as well as the crowded, sedentary conditions they are kept in, makes the cows more likely to get sick.

The same is true for chickens, whose natural diet consists of insects and seeds rather than corn-based chicken feed. They are also often kept in coops so small, and with so many other chickens, that they don't even have room to turn around. And so, to keep these animals healthy, they are also fed large amounts of antibiotics. Because we care so much about getting our food cheaper, animals raised for meat are also fed hormones to make them bulk up quickly. Then we ingest these antibiotics and synthetic hormones when we eat the meat.

According to the comprehensive study done by researchers at the Physicians Committee for Responsible Medicine, and published in 2018 in *Progress in Cardiovascular* Disease, adopting a vegetarian diet can:

- Reduce the risk of death by cardiovascular disease by 40 percent
- Reduce the risk of developing cardiovascular disease by 40 percent
- Fully unblock or partially unblock clogged arteries in as many as 91 percent of patients
- Reduce the risk of high blood pressure by 34 percent

Those are a lot of benefits for just changing your food! Listen, I know how much people love their hamburgers, steaks, bacon, and grilled chicken breasts. I know I'm suggesting something that may feel like a very tall order. I'm not expecting you to read this book and never eat another bite of meat again. But there are gradual steps you can take to reduce your meat consumption and improve the quality and the healthfulness of the meat you do consume.

The first step to changing your relationship to meat is to begin by buying high-quality meat such as organic grass-fed beef and organic pastured chicken and eggs. Animals raised organically aren't subjected to the same level of hormones and antibiotics as those that are raised conventionally. They also have a better nutritional profile than their conventionally-raised counterparts. I know it is more expensive to buy this type of meat; that should help you naturally consume it more thoughtfully and in lower quantities!

At the same time, aim to eat more meatless meals, starting with one meatless meal a week, and working up to the point where perhaps you only eat meat once or twice a week.

Pillar Number Four: Remove the Foods that Don't Agree with Your Body

I'm guessing you can think of at least one food that doesn't agree with you—maybe beans make you gassy, or onions make you burp. But there are likely a few other foods that your body has trouble processing, perhaps even one or two that you eat every day. Until you discover what these foods are, you'll never be able to experience your optimal level of health. It's worth it to do a little digging to see what foods might be irritating you because you may be allergic to them.

Consistently eating foods that your body cannot process compromises your gut health—something you cannot underestimate the importance of. First of all, 90 percent of your immune system resides within your gastrointestinal tract. If your digestion is off, so is your immunity. Meaning, you'll be more susceptible to viruses, more likely to experience inflammation, and at a greater risk for disease, particularly autoimmune disorders.

Beyond that, your gut is your second brain, and the link between gut health and mental health has been well established in scientific literature.[23] The bacteria that live in your gut can produce and regulate levels of neurotransmitters, many of which regulate mood. They communicate with your brain via the vagus nerve, which connects your brain to your internal organs. Anxiety, stress, and depression have all been linked to gut bacteria. And processed, chemical- and hormone-laden foods kill the friendly bacteria in your gut and promote the growth of harmful bacteria. So moving toward a plant-based, whole-food diet, particularly one that is free of irritants, promotes the good bacteria and reduces the bad.

Many people have sensitivities to certain foods and never realize it; they simply become accustomed to the symptoms their food sensitivity is causing. The most common symptoms are brain fog, aches and pains for no apparent reason (meaning, you didn't just do an intense workout), fatigue, lowered immunity, bloating, gas, constipation, and/or diarrhea. When you uncover which foods your body considers to be irritants and remove them, it's like a weight has been lifted off your shoulders.

One of my clients, Renee, was feeling suicidal and starting to wonder if she had bipolar disorder because of her wild mood swings. Then she was diagnosed with celiac disease—a severe allergy to gluten that can only be diagnosed via a blood test. Since then, she's removed gluten and her physical and mental health was turned completely around. She's lost twenty pounds, come off all psychotropic medication, and has had no symptoms of depression.

The best way to determine which foods may be aggravating your digestive system is to do an elimination diet, where you remove all the most common problematic foods—dairy, gluten, eggs, sugar, soy, corn, and shellfish—for ten days, and then slowly reintroduce them into your diet, one at a time, and observe the reactions your body has to them.

If you are daunted by the thought of doing an elimination diet on your own, you can always go see a health-care practitioner who can help you determine which foods aggravate your system. Many naturopathic doctors, functional medicine doctors, and even some chiropractors use muscle testing to see what foods your body has a negative reaction to.

Pillar Number Five: Reduce Your Dependency on Stimulants

So many of us are running on sugar, caffeine, and alcohol—sugar and caffeine to perk us up and help us to have more energy, and alcohol to take the edge off at the end of a long day. I used to drink so much coffee every day because I was so tired from my long commute and stressful job. I had very little time to prepare meals. I would go for long periods without eating anything, and then would need extra energy just to keep going. Then on the weekends I would go out at night and drink a couple glasses of wine, or more, to relax.

The problem with both sugar and caffeine is that they keep your nervous system sympathetically activated. When you drink coffee every day, throughout the day, your system never gets a break. It increases your heart rate and can contribute to an irregular heartbeat. Over time, your body starts to break down.

I know that you are likely legitimately very tired, but that tiredness is a very understandable and natural response to your stressful life. We all need rest to regenerate and recuperate, and if you push your body to go even when it wants to stop, the effort will take its toll.

When you quiet your sympathetic nervous system (which we'll start talking about how to do in Chapter 5), you'll see just how tired you've been, and how much exhaustion you've been covering up with all those stimulants.

One of my clients was a truck driver. He would smoke two packs of cigarettes a day, and drink several cups of coffee to help him stay awake and alert on the road. When he was diagnosed with cancer and had to undergo chemotherapy, he slept most of the day for several months. He hadn't realized just how much he needed the rest. He quit smoking and drinking large amounts of coffee, and now putters around doing things that make him happy every day. I'm happy to report that all that sleeping and those healthy changes have helped him keep his cancer at bay.

Reducing your alcohol intake—or even taking a break from it entirely for a couple of months, if you can—also helps your body get rest. When you drink, your liver has to metabolize that alcohol, which takes a lot of energy and diverts attention from rest and repair while you're sleeping. Also, after you have metabolized the alcohol, it can cause you to wake up in the middle of the night because alcohol is a depressant; so when you sober up, you become energized. In this way, alcohol can impede the number of hours you sleep, as well as the quality of your sleep. If you're going to drink, stick to one glass that you enjoy over a meal, preferably with family or friends. I recommend red wine, which has a high level of antioxidants that can help reduce inflammation.

Pillar Number Six: Follow a Program

By this point, you may be wondering what exactly you're supposed to be eating. I know that changing behaviors and rethinking food can sound good in theory, but hard to implement in real life. That's why I always recommend to my clients that they choose a particular eating strategy that has been shown to reduce risk factors for heart disease, and then stick with it. It takes the guesswork out of deciding what to eat—you don't have to figure anything out or wonder if you're making the right choices. You just follow the plan.

In many cases, the programs I suggest (and outline broadly below) have a component where you can even order food that fits within the guidelines and have it delivered to your door. I realize that there's an expense with this approach, but it is so helpful to give yourself the experience of eating differently. Signing up for a meal service also lets you see how good it feels to be feeding your body foods that are good for it. It can be very motivating, and may very likely help you find the inspiration and dedication to keep following the program on your own after a few weeks or months.

You can get the foods delivered to you and don't have to worry about going to the supermarket. Last night I had a dinner of seitan buffalo wings—seitan is a meat substitute made from wheat gluten—with sautéed peppers and sauce. I only had to heat it up in the microwave and it was delicious and fresh. Generally, if my husband is home he will cook for us, but on the nights when he's at a work function or out with friends, this is my favorite way to eat (no cooking!).

Weight Watchers

Weight Watchers has really stepped up to embrace the digital age. Still based on assigning every food a number of points and counseling followers to keep their points within a certain range, Weight Watchers now has a robust app that you can use on your phone to input your food, keep track of your points, and get recipes. Beyond that, you can still attend in-person meetings, or get support via online chat or phone calls from both professional weight loss mentors, and other members who have used the system to lose weight and keep it off. If you know you do better when you have someone to guide you, Weight Watchers is a great choice that allows you to choose the level of attention you receive and how much you want to pay; as I write this, they have membership options that range between $19.95 and $69.95 a month.

The points system helps you raise awareness of what you're eating and steers you to eat fewer calories, saturated fat, and sugar, while making sure you get plenty of nutritious fruits, vegetables, and whole grains. But it also gives you the flexibility to eat whatever you want, so long as you stick to your allotted total points. I love this program for its ease of use, access to personalized attention, and adaptability—some days you have more time to think about what you're going to eat than others, and Weight Watchers recognizes that and helps you to still stay on track.

Even better, many studies have shown that Weight Watchers is effective at both short-term and long-term weight loss.

DASH Diet

The DASH diet was designed to lower blood pressure based on research by the United States National Institutes of Health. It has been rated "best diet" by *U.S. News and World Report* for the last eight years. It has also been shown to be effective at promoting weight loss, improving depression, stabilizing blood sugar, lowering triglycerides, and treating type 2 diabetes.

The DASH Diet is rich in vegetables, fruits, nuts, beans, whole grains, and seeds, with limited amounts of healthy proteins from low-fat dairy, lean meats, and fish. There are several books that explain the DASH Diet and give lots of recipes and meal ideas. You can also visit www.dashdiet.org to get recipes and meal plans for the original DASH Diet, a version customized to promote weight loss, and a vegetarian version.

Mediterranean Diet

The Mediterranean Diet is named because it follows the breakdown of foods eaten by people who live on the shores of the Mediterranean Sea. It is an eating plan where most of the food is healthy grains, vegetables, or fruit, with plenty of olive oil as accompaniment, herbs and spices for flavor (as opposed to salt), lots of fresh fish and seafood, and only a small amount of dairy and red meat. I especially love that the Mediterranean Diet also emphasizes taking the time to enjoy food with family and friends, and even savor a glass of wine with your meal. As you'll see in pillar number eight, how you eat your food is just as important as what you eat. Food is such a powerful way to bond with others and share parts of your day; it reduces stress, which improves digestion.

The Mediterranean Diet is especially heart healthy. A large review of scientific studies that included over 1.5 million people found that those who followed the principles of the Mediterranean Diet had a significantly lower chance of dying from heart disease than those who did not follow the diet. They also enjoyed a reduction in overall mortality, a lowered risk of dying from cancer, and a decreased risk for developing Parkinson's and Alzheimer's than those who didn't.[24]

Many meal delivery services, such as Blue Apron, Sun Basket, and Plated, offer an option to get only meals that fit with the Mediterranean Diet.

Pillar Number Seven: Develop a Strategy to Minimize Emotional Eating

While it's wonderful to educate yourself about what foods to eat, which to avoid, and why, it's only one piece of the puzzle. As a mental health counselor, I know how many of our food choices have more to do with the emotions we're experiencing than any true physical hunger.

One of my clients, Mindy, is a classic example of an emotional eater. Any time Mindy is upset she reaches for salty, fatty, processed foods and it's taking a toll on her heart health—her blood pressure is high and her heart rate frequently spikes erratically. And Mindy has plenty of opportunities to feel upset. Her mother is eighty-five, and is a master at making Mindy feel guilty. A dutiful daughter (as well as her mother's primary caretaker), Mindy talks to her mom on the phone several times a week. Many times after these phone calls, Mindy is so upset and her heart is racing so much that she will reach for food to help her calm down. One of her favorite things to eat in times of stress are Jax—the cheese puffs that taste so good, but are so terrible for you.

I began helping Mindy untangle her emotional eating by asking her how she felt after she ate the cheese puffs. She reported she felt even worse than when she had started eating—exhausted, disappointed in herself, and so thirsty that no amount of water seemed to quench her thirst.

When you eat because your emotions are getting triggered, it's important to think of a better way to comfort and redirect yourself in the moment. In Mindy's case, we talked about how she can go out for a twenty-minute walk after she hangs up, clear her head and take the edge off her stress, and then come home and drink some ginger and turmeric tea—two herbs that help quell inflammation. It's not easy for Mindy to choose to do the healthy thing, especially in those moments of emotional upset. However, if she is able to step outside, she will have interrupted her pattern and raised her odds of not eating the whole bag of Jax. Making those decisions to stick to her commitment to get healthy helps the emotional triggers not get the best of her.

In a more long-term solution, Mindy is trying to be assertive with her mom and communicating how she feels, instead of letting her mom walk all over her. She's getting much better at speaking from the heart. These changes help reduce the need for comfort eating in the first place. They are also helping to bring down her blood and stabilize her heart rate.

To help you begin to change your relationship with emotional eating, examine what triggers your desire to do it. Is it stress at work? Criticism from a parent? A certain behavior from your partner? Depression? Emotional eating is a coping mechanism. In order to change it, you have to first understand what it is you're coping with, and then choose a more successful and effective way to cope with it.

The Power of Magnesium

Magnesium is a mineral that I often recommend my clients take as a supplement. Magnesium works in tandem with enzymes in your body and plays a role in about 300 different body systems and processes. It helps your muscles relax after contraction, and for that reason it plays a role in blood pressure and heart rate. It is also very helpful for constipation and body aches and pains.

> The problem is, research has found that only 48 percent of Americans are estimated to get enough of it from food. This is troubling, because magnesium deficiency has been associated with all kinds of diseases and conditions, including inflammation, hypertension, atherosclerosis (hardening of the arteries), sudden cardiac death, type 2 diabetes, osteoporosis, asthma, and colon cancer.[25]
>
> One of my clients experiences fairly intense panic and anxiety, and he recently brought me a box of dark chocolates to thank me for recommending magnesium to him. He says it helps with his chronic muscle tightness and helps him sleep at night, which helps reduce his overall anxiety. I generally recommend taking 500–1,000 mg per day, but be sure to talk to your doctor about your dosage.

Pillar Number Eight: How You Eat Is Just As Important As What You Eat

When I was growing up, my father came home at 6:30 every night. My mom would cook a gourmet meal, and we'd sit down together at the table. Before we ate, we'd say grace. We'd thank God for the food, and my mother for preparing it. It was an important ritual even though I didn't always see it that way—many nights I just wanted to dig in! Looking back on it now, I see how it elevated dinner into an opportunity to feel grateful and connected to one another, and to a higher power.

However, I don't do anything near that elaborate on a regular basis. My husband and I work different schedules, so we often don't even eat together. But when we have people over, we hold hands at the table and I thank my husband for cooking (he does almost all our cooking). We express thanks for the food. We thank each other for taking the time to be together. When we express thanks, it creates such a different feeling.

It's a simple truth that eating is about so much more than just food. We've lost that sense of appreciation for the food that fuels us and nourishes us. Now, we mostly try to eat whatever we can get on a plate as quickly as possible so that we can get on to the next thing.

I'm not saying that I think we all need to get back to having home-cooked, gourmet meals every night, or saying grace. You will appreciate your food more if you take a moment to acknowledge where your food comes from before you eat it. This will also help you break the habit of rushing to get the food down. Pausing to take a few deep breaths before you dive in helps reduce your stress levels, which makes you able to better digest food and puts you in a more present state of mind so that you can enjoy your food more. You'll be able to better savor the sight, smells, and taste of it. Clients often tell me that when they pay more attention to what they're eating, they feel more satisfied and less likely to overeat.

When you have more time—like on the weekend—or when you have friends or family over for dinner, you could each take a moment to say one thing you're thankful for. There is something healing about taking time to feel and express your gratitude.

The food doesn't have to be homemade for you to be thankful for it. I definitely give thanks for the foods I heat up from the meal service I use. I'm especially thankful that I didn't have to cook it, and that I don't have a kitchen full of dishes waiting for me after I eat!

Pillar Number Nine: Make Splurging the Exception, Not the Rule

I realize that everything I've recommended in this chapter might be setting off alarm bells in your mind, making you feel that no level of health is worth it if you can never again have an ice cream cone, or eat your Mom's apple pie, or enjoy the BBQ rib recipe you've spent years perfecting.

The good news is that you don't have to be 100 percent perfect. This is a very good thing, because no one can be 100 percent perfect! Even if 25 percent of the time you are eating all the feel-good foods you love, and 75 percent of the time you're sticking to nutritious whole foods, your health will still dramatically improve. I tell my clients who are convinced that changing their diet completely is too hard, or too much of a sacrifice, to "cheat" on the weekends and go back to their diets on Monday.

Even I will splurge every once in a while and have a bag of Doritos. So have your barbecue ribs on Saturday. But come Monday, go back to your mostly plant-based wholefoods. I can promise you that when you give yourself long enough to adapt to your new eating style, you will feel so much better that you won't see it as a sacrifice. You'll stop thinking about what you are giving up, and starting recognizing how much you're getting.

CHAPTER 5

EXERCISE FOR HEART HEALTH

As important as food is to your heart health, it's only going to go so far to improve your heart if you don't pair it with exercise. It's a fundamental truth that our bodies were designed to move. Being sedentary all day, every day, knocks the body out of balance to the point that the lack of physical activity is not only a risk factor, but also a predictor of heart disease.

It makes sense. After all, your heart is a muscle—a muscle that never stops working and that needs conditioning to function at its best. If you're having trouble carrying heavy groceries, you need to strengthen your arm muscles. If you are seeking more energy and better health in any area of your life, you need to strengthen your heart muscle.

The Heart Benefits of Exercise

Your heart exists to support your body; it empowers every cell by delivering blood, oxygen, and nutrients. It also fuels every movement you make. This relationship between your heart and the rest of your body is not a one-way street; your body also supports your heart. If you aren't moving your body regularly, you are creating conditions for your heart to stagnate.

In fact, people who are sedentary are almost twice as likely to get heart disease as people who are active—twice as likely!

The fact that you can cut your risk of heart disease in half by moving more makes exercise as effective as any prescription. It's a pill you can give yourself, for free, with very few negative side effects (so long as you don't decide to practically kill yourself with a workout that your body isn't yet equipped to handle). Best of all, it improves not just your heart health, but also your emotional, mental, and spiritual health.

I think you know by now that I am a huge fan of reducing unnecessary stress in your life. But there is such a thing as *beneficial* stress—something that challenges you to grow beyond your current edge, something that may be difficult but that helps you become stronger. In your life, that may be having a difficult conversation with a family member that opens the door to having a more fulfilling relationship. Or maybe it's giving a big presentation at work that makes your knees knock, but also helps you get that promotion you've been seeking. Exercise is a beneficial stressor for your heart—even moderate exercise challenges your heart and inspires it to grow stronger.

At the most basic level, moving your body gets your heart pumping and increases your circulation, which aids your heart in delivering blood to every cell. In this way, it makes you more alive. Beyond that, exercise is an important part of the mind-body connection. If you're not feeling well physically, then you're not going to feel well mentally, and vice versa. Physical health and mental health benefit from each other.

One of my clients recently lost her husband of thirty-five years to pancreatic cancer. She has been finding it hard just to get out of bed; she'd rather curl up with her thoughts and ruminate about her loss. My first recommendation was designed to get her brain engaged in something other than thinking about her sadness. I suggested that she write out the story of her romance with her husband, starting with when they first met. My second suggestion was that she go on at least a short walk every day. Moving your body also helps you move through difficult emotions.

This client has two dogs, so she has even more of a reason to go on a walk at least once a day. However, it was something she used to do with her husband, she had been avoiding it at first. Now she's taking twenty-minute walks with her dogs four days a week. It's been a way for her to feel connected to her husband as she's tending to her heart health. She's taking it day by day, but every day she walks, she says she feels much better.

Like this client of mine, you don't have to train for a marathon, or do something that pushes your limits, in order to reap important mental, emotional, and physical benefits. Even getting up out of your chair to take a walk for ten minutes once or twice a day counts as exercise.

Believe me, I know how hard it can seem to find these extra minutes. Every time I bring up exercise with my therapy clients, they get a panicked look in their eye that says *I can't commit to doing one more thing!* And I always bring it up; exercise is part of every one of my clients' plans. It's that important.

Everyone has the ability to be more active. If a client is physically disabled, I prescribe chair yoga and stretching. If they are insanely busy, we get out their calendar and go over it together, looking for the opportunities that are hiding in plain sight. There is *something* you can do, and your body, mind, and spirit will thank you for it.

The irony is that regular exercise energizes you. It helps you do everything in your life more effectively and efficiently. In that way, it's like it creates time for you.

Some of the more specific benefits of exercise include:

- **Managing your weight.** The food you eat has a huge impact on your weight—so resist the temptation to think you can exercise your way out of a bad diet. But moving more does burn calories and raise your metabolism (particularly if you are doing strength or resistance training). It can also improve digestion and help to clear your head so that you are less likely to eat emotionally. Over time, all these benefits mean you are more apt to avoid the weight gain that so many assume is unavoidable as we age. Exercise also makes it easier to maintain the weight loss that may result from improving your diet.

Beyond the self-esteem boost that losing weight can provide, shedding excess pounds also lowers strain on the heart and removes a major risk factor for heart disease and stroke.

- **Promoting mental and cognitive health.** Exercise releases many feel-good chemicals, such as endorphins and dopamine. Endorphins are the magical clarity-promoting and pain-reducing neurotransmitters responsible for a "runner's high." Dopamine is the pleasure hormone that is often reduced in the presence of depression. The chemical also reduces levels of hormones that perpetuate chronic stress, such as cortisol. Because of these chemical changes, when you move your body, you think more clearly. Your spirits lift. You get a sense of clarity on your life and what you want to do next that is much, much harder to find if you spend all your time sitting in a chair or lying on the couch.
- **Improving cholesterol levels.** Exercise reduces LDL, or "bad," cholesterol and boosts your HDL, or "good," cholesterol. This means that your arteries become less prone to clogging, and your heart has better access to blood flow.
- **Lowering blood pressure and resting heart rate.** When you move your body, you increase circulation and dilation of your blood vessels. This in turn lowers blood pressure and improves the flexibility of your arteries (the hardening of the arteries is a hallmark of heart disease). This challenge to your heart also helps it grow stronger and work more efficiently when you aren't moving, so that your resting heart rate comes down. This means your heart is required to beat thousands and thousands of times less over time, and this helps preserve its integrity and promote its longevity.
- **Improving blood sugar.** When you move your body, your muscles take glucose from your bloodstream to use as energy. This leads to lower blood sugar levels, which in turn lowers your

insulin levels. Since insulin is a hormone that tells the body to store extra calories as fat, lowering your blood sugars also helps regulate your weight, as well as reduces the risk of type 2 diabetes. If you already have diabetes, exercise helps you regulate your blood sugar levels naturally.

- **Strengthening your muscles.** Exercise forces your muscles to adapt and grow stronger. This is especially important as you get older, as we start to lose muscle mass—as much as five percent per year—after age thirty. And having a healthy amount of muscle mass means that your everyday life is easier. You can carry your groceries and lift your kids (or your grandkids). Also, the more muscle mass you have, the higher your metabolism is likely to be, which makes it easier to prevent weight gain over time—a good thing, because being overweight strains your heart. Exercise also forces your muscles to get more efficient at drawing oxygen out of the blood so that the heart has to work less hard to deliver oxygen to the muscles, even when you are at rest.
- **Helping you quit smoking.** If you smoke, you know that you probably feel its negative effects most when you exert yourself and it gets harder to breathe. The fitter you become, the more you can appreciate your ability to breathe deeply and easily, and the more inspiration you have to stop doing anything that impedes that. Smoking is one of the biggest risk factors for heart disease because it harms your blood vessels.
- **Reducing stress.** Try this: the next time you feel stressed, take a walk outside for just a few minutes. You'll see for yourself that exercise brings your stress levels down.
- **Lowering inflammation.** The beneficial stressor of exercise helps retrain and strengthen your immune system so that it isn't triggered as much, which brings inflammation down. Since inflammation is a root contributor to so many diseases,

including heart disease, this is one of the most important benefits that exercise provides.
- **Creating an upward spiral of health.** When you exercise, you build your muscles and your bones, and this in turn enables you to exercise more and take on more fulfilling activities. It also empowers you to be more confident and competent in your own life—it makes it easier to carry your groceries, pick up your kids or grandkids, and prevent the falls that can cause injuries that limit your ability to move your body.

All these benefits are yours for the taking! You have to do the work, it's true, but it takes less work than you think. When you see how good it feels to get more movement in your life, it really won't feel like work.

How Much Exercise—and What Kind—Is Right for You?

According to the American Heart Association's 2013 exercise standards, "Exercise can be viewed as a preventative medical treatment, 'like a pill.'" The trick is to customize the plan for you—your abilities, your likes, and your life.

What is it that you're interested in doing? Do you want something easy and doable? Walking would be a great choice. Is there something you used to enjoy and want to get back to, or maybe something new you've been interested in trying? Doing something you enjoy is great motivation, you just have to make sure you start back slowly so that you don't overdo it and injure yourself.

Again, you don't need to sign up for a triathlon. I'm not really talking about getting into the best shape of your life; I'm talking about simply moving your body more. Science tells us that that's all you really need to do to significantly improve your heart health.

According to a 2015 scientific review of twenty-two studies that included more than 320,000 adults, published in *The American Journal of Medicine*, even a really modest level of activity—as little as one hour of walking or gardening per week—was associated with reduced rates of heart attack, stroke, and overall mortality. One of the studies included in the review found that people who did some kind of moderate exercise for only fifteen minutes a day lived an average of three years longer than people who got no exercise.[26]

So please, start slow. You may discover a love of fitness that you didn't know you had and want to challenge yourself more and more, which would be great! But you don't need intensity unless you absolutely want it. I'd much rather you start taking short little walks, and then gradually take on more of a challenge, than you go to the gym and lift a bunch of weights you're not ready for. You could end up either pulling a muscle or incapacitating yourself with soreness, and decide exercise isn't for you. You're aiming for consistency—both in your level of effort, and in the progress you make.

Just as with a prescription, you have to put yourself on a schedule. You want to make sure you are getting at least twenty minutes of moderate aerobic exercise, which could be as simple as walking—not leisurely ambling along, but walking like you've got somewhere to be—at least three times a week. Four or five, or even seven days a week, is better. However, if you go from sedentary to walking three times a week, that is a fabulous place to start.

It's also helpful to add in one or two days of some kind of strength training, whether that's bodyweight exercises such as a push-ups and squats, or lifting weights, even if they are light. You can even use soup cans or jugs of water as weights. Building more muscle mass raises your metabolism and strengthens your bones, warding off osteoporosis as you age. Whenever you can, add in a little stretching to improve your flexibility; it will help you ward off aches and pains, and make you less prone to injuries and falls as you get older.

I love walking because all you need is a good pair of shoes; you can go right out your front door, and it doesn't cost money or have to happen at a specific time. My second favorite way to get aerobic exercise is to enroll in some kind of scheduled class. If you can just get yourself there at the appointed time, whether it's a spinning, dancing, Pilates, or yoga class, you know you'll get your exercise. The only hard part is showing up.

I find that when I work out in the morning, I feel more energized all day. When I don't, my stress levels are higher and my energy is lower, which makes it less likely that I'll work out later. Another strategy that works for a lot of my clients is to take an active midday break—walking just before, or just after eating lunch. It clears your mind, refreshes you, and helps you have a more productive afternoon. Some people really just don't have any time to themselves until they are done with work, so evenings are their best time of day to exercise. I promise you, the time is there if you look for it. The average American spends over ten hours a day on screens—if you have that much time for watching and scrolling, I promise you have twenty minutes for movement. Once you do those twenty minutes, you're more likely to keep going, or do more later in the day.

I encourage my clients not to think about exercise on a daily basis, but to plan their exercise a week at a time. At the beginning of every week, look at your schedule and decide what you'll do and when. Make sure your exercise clothes are clean, and set them out so you can see them— you can even sleep in them if that will help you actually exercise as soon as you wake up.

After each time you exercise, pause for just a minute before you head back into your day and check in with how you feel. When you take time to notice the benefits exercise provides, it will build your resolve to do it the next time it seems like you just don't have the time or energy.

At the end of every week, check in on how you did—did you exercise as many times as you planned to? If not, ask yourself why, and then use that information to adjust your schedule for next week.

I have another client who just had her second child, so she has a two-year-old and a three-month-old baby. She's hormonal and having symptoms of postpartum depression. She really needed some time alone to take care of herself, but she had been thinking it just wasn't feasible. Together, we sat down and looked at her schedule. She developed a plan to give her husband an hour to do whatever he'd like from 4:00–5:00 p.m., and then she gets 5:00–6:00 p.m. to do what she wants to do. Then they have dinner as a family. The time really is there if you'll just look and allow yourself to entertain possibilities.

My Favorite Form of Exercise

It's no secret that I am a huge fan and student of yoga. I teach a weekly yoga class, and also walk many of my clients through a few poses in their counseling sessions. Because I wrote my doctoral dissertation on using yoga poses and the chakras to heal the body and the mind, this is one of my favorite portions of the work I do with clients. We get on the yoga mat and they have an emotional release, which helps them think more clearly and make better decisions about how they respond to the stressors in their life. The more they practice, the better able they are to hear their intuition and make changes that lead to greater happiness and fulfillment.

Yoga is an ancient practice that is a wonderful form of fitness—it combines cardio, strength training, and flexibility in one package. And it is so much more. It encourages you to really be in the moment by inviting the mind into the body, which promotes your mental, emotional, and spiritual health, in addition to the physical conditioning it provides. In fact, the ancient texts that describe yoga, *The Yoga Sutras*, state that "yoga is the cessation of the fluctuation of the mind." By doing these physical postures, you create the conditions for your thoughts to settle down and create the quiet you need to hear your wisdom and intuition.

If you choose only one form of exercise to practice, yoga would be a great choice. Doing it on your own four times a week is a beautiful way to take care of your heart. Research published in the *European Journal of Preventive Cardiology*[27] has even found that yoga has a similar effect to other forms of exercise when it comes to reducing several key risk factors for heart disease, including improving cholesterol, weight loss, lower blood pressure, and reduced heart rate.

Another study by researchers at the University of Kansas found that doing yoga twice a week for three months reduced symptoms of depression and anxiety, lowered blood pressure and heart rate, and significantly reduced incidences of disturbed heart rate in patients with atrial fibrillation—a form of heart disease that affects millions of Americans and that causes rapid and/or irregular heartbeat.

While these are powerful benefits for your physical heart, I believe that yoga is truly remarkable for its positive effects on your metaphorical heart. Known as the *anahata chakra* in Sanskrit, the energy that emanates from your heart starts with self-love, and from there radiates out into love for others—our family, our partners, our communities, and our fellow humans.

Because yoga gives you the opportunity to really pay attention to who you are and what you're feeling in the moment, it helps you know yourself better and accept who you are, which are both important parts of loving yourself. That self-love can then fuel your love for others. So, it's not just your health you're promoting when you do yoga, it's everyone around you.

Poses for a Home Yoga Practice

Here are the poses I recommend to my clients that I teach in my classes, and that I do on my own. Done in a sequence and repeated a few times, these poses make up what's known as a Sun Salutation, a practice that is designed to warm up and strengthen the body, while also clearing the mind and opening the heart to a new day. They add up to a cardiovascular workout that strengthens the heart, the lungs, and all the muscles of the body. When you do the Sun Salutation, you'll notice your heart beating faster, and feel a pleasant warmth emanating from the inside out.

Sun Salutation

Start off in a comfortable, seated, cross-legged position. Close your eyes or gaze down at the tip of your nose. Breathe in through your nose, and out through your nose. With each breath, feel your hips, lower back, middle back, upper back, shoulders, arms, and neck relax.

Next, fold forward as far as you can, walking your hands out in front of you on the floor to open up your low back and hips. Return to sitting upright and change the cross of your legs so that the other one is in front, and then fold forward again.

After a few breaths, return to sitting upright, then come onto your hands and knees with your hands shoulder-width apart and knees hip-width apart for **cat-cow stretching**. Inhale while you arch your spine and drop your chin to your chest like an angry cat. Then, as you exhale, drop your belly down toward the floor, like a cow with full udders, as you lift your chin to look up. Repeat this cycle of arching upward, and then releasing the belly down for three or four cycles. End in a flat back position.

Next, move your hips back and sit your hips on your heels for a **cat stretch**. Reach your arms out, walking your fingers out as far as possible while not allowing your arms to touch the mat to get a nice stretch in your upper arms, shoulders, and upper back.

After two or three breaths here, slide your nose along the mat until you are fully stretched out on your stomach. Place your hands underneath your armpits, tuck your elbows in by your side, and bring your heels together. Pressing into your palms, come up into **cobra pose** with your hips and legs resting on the floor, and your head, chest, and abdomen lifting up toward the ceiling, making your arms as straight as you can mange. Take two or three breaths here, reaching your chest forward, through your arms.

Next, tuck your toes under while making sure your feet are hip-width apart, and lift your hips up off the floor to come into **down dog**. Your hands should be flat to the mat, fingers spread apart, and arms lined up next to your ears. Press from your hands to your hips, and from your hips to your heels. Keep your legs straight and stay for two or three breaths. (It doesn't matter if your heels reach the floor or not.)

Then, lift your right leg up into the air and swing it forward to bring your right foot to the mat inbetween your hands in a **lunge**. (If you need to modify this movement, drop your left knee to the mat, and step your right foot in between your hands instead of swinging it forward). Then bring your left foot to meet the right. Keep your knees bent and your head down to rest in a **forward bend** for a breath or two. Straighten your legs very slowly—it is okay if your hands do not stay on the mat or touch your toes. The goal is to keep the weight of your body over the balls of your feet, with your legs straight, reaching your tailbone to the ceiling or sky. Try to relax here—you can cross your arms and hold on to opposite elbows if your fingers don't reach the floor—and not force yourself further down.

Stay folded forward for two or three breaths, then bend your knees, tuck your chin into your chest, and slowly uncurl one vertebra at a time, until you are standing upright in **mountain pose**. The yogis say that this fundamental standing position is a complete yoga practice contained in one pose. When you concentrate on all the physical points that add up to this pose, it will certainly help still the fluctuations of your mind.

To do **mountain pose**, stand tall and feel the weight of your body balanced over the balls of your feet. Tuck your tailbone in to protect your lower back. Now, imagine there is a ball of energy coming from the soles of your feet, and that ball of energy is moving up over your ankles, shins, calves, kneecaps, and thighs. Feel it continue to rise up through the hips, and as it travels further up, it engages your core and lifts the sternum so that the waist thins. As the ball of energy continues to rise, feel it soften your shoulders, lengthen your neck, and lift the crown of your head to the ceiling. As you stand at your tallest and most grounded, let go of any tension in your arms and fingers. Then let that ball of energy drop down through the spine, the backs of your legs, and all the way back down to the soles of your feet.

Next, bring your hands together, palms touching, in front of your heart center in prayer position. Lift them up over your head and separate your hands to shoulder-width apart. Lift the chin and the chest, and drop your shoulders to come back into a tiny **standing backbend**.

Return to standing upright, bring your palms back together and lower them along the front of the body as you bend forward into a **forward bend** with straight legs. Bend your knees and bring your fingertips to the floor. Line up your fingers and your toes, and then step your right foot back into **lunge**. Then step your left foot back to come into **down dog**. Stay for a breath or two.

Bring your knees down to the floor and bring your hips back to your heels for **cat stretch**, **stay** for a breath. Slide your nose along the mat to come up into **cobra** for another breath. Then tuck your toes under and lift your hips up while coming into **down dog**.

On an inhale, step the right foot forward between your hands, and then the left foot, to come into **forward bend**. Extend your spine forward so your back is flat, bend your knees, reach your arms out in front of you so that they are parallel to each other, and then press into your feet as you rise up to standing with your arms reaching up over your head. Keep your hands shoulder-width apart. Lift your chest and chin upward so that you come into a small standing **back bend**.

Return to standing upright and bring your hands together into prayer position over your head. Lower your hands to your chest, and then all the way down toward the floor as you come into **forward bend** again with straight legs. Pause for a breath, then bend your knees, bring your fingertips to the floor in line with your toes, and send the left foot back into **lunge**. Follow with your right foot, and move into **down dog**.

Lift up onto your toes and lower your knees to the floor, reaching back into **cat stretch**, and then slide your nose along the mat to come forward into **cobra**.

Curl your toes under and come back into **down dog**. Send the left foot forward to land between your hands, and then right foot follows. Fold into **forward bend**. Then rise all the way up with arms lifted straight, and come into a standing **back bend**. End by standing in **mountain pose** with your hands in prayer in front of your heart.

Repeat the entire sequence for a total of three to five times. After your final **mountain pose**, come down into a **forward bend**, step your right foot and then left foot back into **down dog**. Lift up onto your toes, bring your knees to the floor and move your hips back to rest on your heels with your forehead resting on the floor. Arms should be wrapped around your legs with palms facing up in **child's pose**. If you can't get your forehead to the mat, make fists out of your hands and place them under your forehead. Stay for a few breaths.

Next, curl your chin into your chest and slowly begin to sit up, uncurling one vertebra at a time until you are sitting on your shins, toes untucked, in what's known as **thunderbolt pose**. Shift your hips to the floor next to your left heel, and swing your legs out in front of you so that you are sitting in a straight-legged position. Bend your knees and hold onto the backs of your thighs with your hands, then tuck your chin into your chest and slowly roll onto your back with your knees still bent and thighs curled in toward your chest.

When you're on your back, extend your legs out straight along the floor and separate your feet so that your left foot reaches the left edge of your mat, and the right foot reaches the right edge of the mat (feet are hip-width apart). Let your arms rest on the floor alongside your torso with the palms facing up. Tuck your chin in a tiny bit, relax your jaw, and close your eyes. Now you are in **corpse pose**.

Stay here, focusing your attention on your breath, for up to five minutes. This final pose is where we reap all the benefits of the yoga practice. It invites the mind into the body, helps relax the muscles, and releases tension in the body and the mind. It's a restorative pose that helps your entire being rejuvenate itself.

Breathing for Better Heart Health

Pranayama, which translates to "breath control," is a sister science and practice to yoga. It is designed to fortify the body, clear the mind, and create a state of physiological calm where healing can take place. In the relaxed state that these breathing techniques create, you can more clearly hear what's on your mind. These breathing techniques are an excellent tool to help you make decisions and recover from setbacks. Hillary Clinton spoke openly about using the pranayama practice of alternate nostril breathing to help her recuperate after the brutal campaign season, and to process her loss. No matter what your politics are, they can help you heal your body and bolster your heart, too.

Alternate Nostril (*Nadi Shodhana*)

This breathing exercise balances the right and left hemispheres of the brain, fostering whole-brain function. It's both integrating and grounding. It also creates a deep sense of well-being on the physical, mental, and emotional level. It can be helpful for headaches, migraines, and other stress-related symptoms.

When you begin by inhaling on the left and exhaling on the right, the effect is calming and helps you get rid of unwanted negative emotions and stress—an excellent way to relax before bed. Conversely, when you inhale right and exhale left, this technique lends clarity and helps to create a positive mood, so that you can focus on what is important.

How to do it: Sit in a comfortable seated position with your spine tall, crown of your head lifting to the ceiling. You can keep your eyes open or closed. Bring the right hand, palm facing in, in front of your face. Use the thumb of the right hand to close the right nostril gently, and fully inhale through the left nostril. When you can't inhale any more, release the pressure on your right nostril, and close the left nostril with your right ring finger. Exhale, slowly and completely, through the right nostril. Without changing your finger position, inhale through the right nostril. Then release the left nostril, close the right nostril with your right thumb, and exhale through the left nostril. Continue for at least ten full breaths, alternating nostrils after each inhalation.

Victorious Breath (*Ujjayi*)

Because it increases circulation and lung capacity, ujjayi (ooh-jye-ee), or **victorious breath**, is heating and detoxifying to the body. It is also very energizing, and promotes mental focus and calm. I like to use this breathing when I want to steady myself before a big day, or to replenish myself after a hard day at work.

How to do it: Begin in a comfortable, cross-legged seated position. Relax your body, particularly your jaw and your tongue, and close your eyes. Start to notice the air of your inhalations passing through your windpipe. On your exhalations, slightly contract the back of your throat, as you do when you whisper. Direct the breath to travel over your vocal cords, and across the back of your throat. Keep your mouth closed, but your lips soft. Your exhales should make a sound like Darth Vader when you've got it right. As you become comfortable with maintaining the constriction during your exhalations, start to do it while inhaling, too. You will notice your breath making an "ocean" sound, softly moving in and out like ocean waves.

Your breathing should be audible to you, but not so loud that someone standing several feet away can hear it. Concentrate on the sound of your breath, allowing it to soothe your mind. Let your inhalations fill your lungs to their fullest expansion. Completely release the air during your exhalations.

Start by practicing ujjayi for five minutes while you are seated. For deeper meditation, increase your time to fifteen minutes. Eventually, you can also use it continuously throughout your yoga practice, syncing your movements to each inhale and exhale—it supercharges the benefits of your practice when you do.

Sukhasana

Cat-Cow Stretch – Chakravakasana

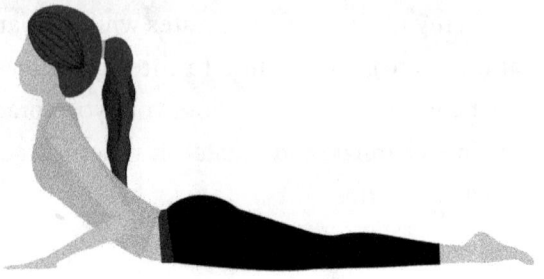

Cobra Pose – Bhujangasana

Lunge Kneeling

Lunge – Anjaneyasana

Down Dog – Adho Mukha Svanasana

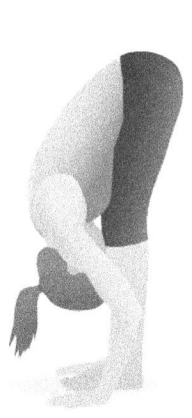

Forward Bend – Uttanasana

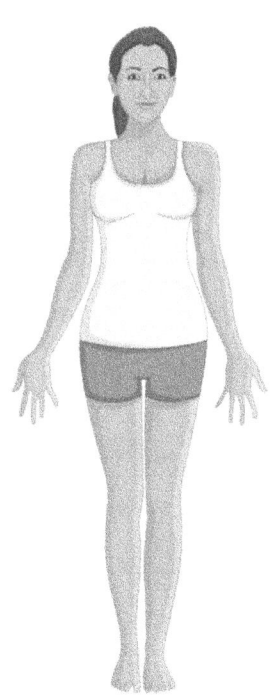

Mountain Pose – Tadasana

Standing Pose – Anuvittasana

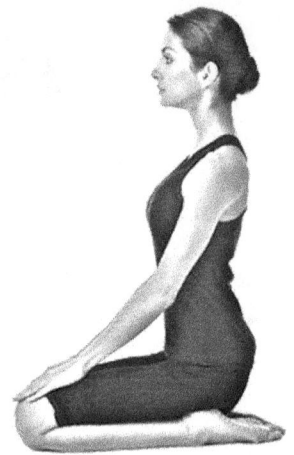
Thunderbolt Pose – Vajrasana

Cat Stretch – Active Child's Pose

Child Pose – Balasana

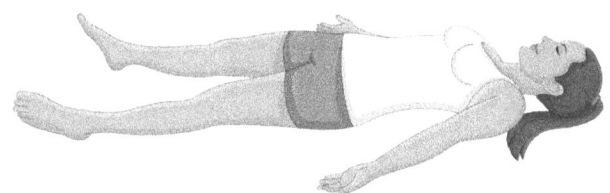

Corpse Pose – Savasana

CHAPTER 6

LIFESTYLE CHANGES FOR A HEALTHIER HEART

As important as diet and exercise are for your health, they can only go so far. If you are eating the healthiest diet in the world and exercising most days of the week, your heart will still be compromised if you hate your job, have challenging family relationships, or both. Many of the people I see in my office are struggling with one or two of these vital parts of life.

Work and family can feel like things that are difficult—if not impossible—to improve; you need money from your job to survive, and your family is your family—there's nothing you can do about it. Or at least, that's what many of us try to tell ourselves. But you have so much power to change these areas for the better.

In this chapter, you'll learn exactly how to make it so that your work life and your family life support your heart health. I also cover another part of your life that can have a huge impact on your overall health, happiness, and fulfillment (and a part of life the vast majority of health practitioners never address)—your hobbies. When you take the information in this chapter to heart (no pun intended), you will be able to remedy some of the biggest emotional drains on heart health.

Is Your Work Situation Lifting You Up, or Dragging You Down?

In order for our hearts to be healthy, we need to feel connected to the work we do. Why? Viewed through the lens of the chakra system, the heart center is about loving yourself and then offering that love to others outside of you—whether they are part of your family, community, or your clientele. In addition to being a source of income, your work is an important outlet for how you offer love and care to others. If you don't feel love for the work you do, and the people you do it for and with, it's going to weigh on your heart.

Don't get me wrong, I love financial security as much as the next person. But if the only positive thing your job provides is a steady paycheck—and nearly everything else about it causes you stress—it may be harming your health bottom line.

Together let's talk through the two main ways to feel more connected to your work; look for more meaning in the job you have, or look for a new job.

After all, the heart craves knowing that you are creating a positive impact in the lives of others.

Option 1 for Improving Your Work Life: Seek to Create More Meaning

Creating meaning doesn't mean you must have a job that is focused on solving the world's problems; you can find meaning in a wide range of jobs. For example, one of my patients, Claire, is a medical assistant, helping a doctor in private practice. In one of our early sessions, Claire confided, "I know it pays the bills, but it's killing me to go to that job every day." She may have been exaggerating, but only a little. Claire was demonstrating symptoms of depression and anxiety, both of which are associated with heart disease, particularly in women. This job itself probably wasn't killing her, but it was creating the conditions that result in an overtaxed and vulnerable heart. Sharing that perspective with Claire provided her with the motivation to make changes to her work life.

Together, we looked for aspects of Claire's job that she could find meaning in—such as how it could pay for some additional schooling, and how it allowed her to help others. Thinking of it that way did help Claire feel less depressed, and it inspired her to focus on being there to assist the doctors and patients who visit the office. She also felt inspired to start looking at educational options that would open up a more rewarding career path for her. We broke this process down into very doable steps, of spending an hour a week researching options online, and aiming to have at one conversation at least every other week with people whose jobs Claire found intriguing. In this way, she would have some real-world stories to guide her on choosing an area of study that would result in work she actually enjoyed.

To look for the meaning in your own work, do an inventory of the aspects that have positive benefits for you. I suggest asking yourself the following questions:

- How does your job help you contribute to something you value?
- What does the money you earn make possible in your life?
- How are your relationships there nurturing you?

There may be more facets to appreciate about your job than you are currently aware of, because you are so focused on the fact that you hate it.

Option 2 for Improving Your Work Life: Look for a New Job

If you've tried looking for the meaning and you just can't find it, it's time to start looking for different opportunities so that you don't feel trapped.

I have a client, Debra, who personifies that situation so many of us face: having a decent job that drains our well-being. From the outside, Debra seems to have it all. She has a high-level position at her job. She makes a ton of money. She's well-respected and well-liked by her colleagues. She has two gorgeous children and a healthy marriage. And yet Debra feels disconnected from her work—she doesn't enjoy it at all. The work also comes with a lot of stress on its own that is made worse by the fact that she doesn't like her job. It's gotten to the point that she's been having near-constant anxiety, and frequent panic attacks.

When Debra came to see me, we spent a lot of our first session talking about how conflicted she felt. On one hand, she had no personal attachment to the company's mission, and that lack of connection felt like it was, as she said, "sucking the life out of me." On the other hand, she needed the money and feared she wouldn't be able to earn as much somewhere else. (Sound familiar?)

Debra had already tried everything she could think of to derive more meaning from her work, but she felt strongly that her values didn't jibe with the company's mission. So, we started talking about her beginning to look for a new job.

I know what a big task that sounds like, but I always counsel my clients to start with baby steps:

- Get your resume together.
- Update your LinkedIn profile.
- Tell a few trusted people that you are looking.
- Start to look at job listings online.
- Do one thing every week or so, and see what happens.

Taking action will feel much better than feeling trapped. There's no harm in looking; you really only stand to gain.

When Debra started doing these things, she started feeling better immediately. She said; "It makes me feel like I'm not trapped in this life that I hate and don't want to do anymore." She hadn't touched her LinkedIn profile in five years. Just the experience of going back and looking at her accomplishments, and knowing that she's putting herself out there in a thoughtful way, boosted her confidence that she could find something else. Debra hadn't even thought about doing these things because she's felt like she's had to stay in her job.

I'm not suggesting you take on another position that sounds good on paper, but that you'll also hate going to every day. I am suggesting that you look for a job that speaks to your heart. It could be any job; I've had patients who work at Stop & Shop and love it. Of course, making enough money to live comfortably is good for your heart, too. You don't have to take a vow of poverty in order to be happy. Just remember, a job is about more than the title and money. It's about how you put your skills, talents, and values to use in the world. Knowing that you are being of use, contributing to something you believe in, and being valued for that contribution, is priceless. It makes you happier and healthier, and those two things are vital for true wealth.

To help guide you to a job that feeds your heart, begin by asking yourself:

- What do I love doing?
- What things do I care about?
- What demonstrable skills do I have, whether I honed them in my schooling, my past and current jobs, raising my family, or in my community work?

Everything you've done up until this point—whether you were paid for it or not—counts. Taking stock of your skills and your competences builds your confidence and makes you feel more hopeful that the right job opportunity for you exists.

Benjamin Franklin said that nothing can be certain in this world except for death and taxes. I want to add something else to that list: change. Change is a given, because everything in life is impermanent. While that may sound scary to some, change is a good thing because monotony can wear you down over time. In fact, change can be profoundly healing. It breaks you out of rigid patterns and stimulates your brain; getting up and going to the same place every day can be soul-killing.

Of course, change can also be really scary, particularly when you have dependents. You do want to carefully consider your options. But if your work situation isn't feeling good anymore, you've lost the connection to it that you once had, and you can't find a way to appreciate what it's offering you, there's no harm in looking for other opportunities.

I know how daunting it can feel to change your work situation. I recently closed the office that housed my practice for thirteen years, and transitioned to working out of two different offices that are closer to the new house where my husband and I moved. I also started offering tele-therapy, which I can do from home.

It wasn't an easy choice to close an office where I'd spent so much time building a clientele. With any change, there is risk involved. But risk cuts both ways—there's also the risk of not trying something that could work out to my advantage. This change in my business could bring me to a different level of income (since I am offering my clients more options) and add more meaning to my life (since I'll spend less time commuting, leaving me more time to pursue things that are meaningful to me).

Being honest with yourself and knowing what you care about is how you create a job situation that you love, and that's good for your heart. I promise you there is an opportunity out there for you to love what you do and help others, while also being true to yourself.

Make Time for Hobbies

What happens when you're off the clock is just as important as what you do for work when it comes to happiness, fulfillment, and ultimately, heart health. As important as it is to weed out the things that cause you upset, stress, and disconnect, it's just as important to add things in that make you feel inspired, happy, and creative. Pursuing a hobby is a great way to do that.

I get that you might be surprised to have a book about heart health tell you to spend more time doing hobbies; I know they can seem frivolous. When I ask my clients what they do for hobbies, they often look at me like I've grown an extra head, like, *I don't have time for hobbies!*

But hobbies are incredibly important because they help you spend more time in an energetic state that comes when you are doing something simply because you love it, and that is absolutely relevant and vital to your heart health. Hobbies are how adults experience the power of play, which is just as important for grown-ups as it is for kids. Whether you are playing with how you'll lay out a page in your scrapbook, or playing Frisbee, allowing yourself to do something just for the fun of it elicits feel-good neurochemicals, such as dopamine (which is associated with a rewarding feeling) and norepinephrine (which helps us pay attention and learn, it also helps our brains stay adaptable). Better yet, these feel-good chemicals don't require a prescription. That means that not only are they free, but you don't need to go see a doctor to get them. You hold the power to make yourself feel better.

It really doesn't matter what your hobby is—you may enjoy gardening, hiking, knitting, playing tennis, playing music, skiing, doing crossword puzzles, cooking, or collecting stamps. The only key is that the hobby is something you truly enjoy. Activities that feed your soul increase your enjoyment in life, and that nourishes your body, mind, and spirit. It takes you out of the busyness of your head and gives you much-needed time off from being productive, which helps you relax and allows your thoughts to settle down.

I'll bet you've had an experience—even if it was years ago—of being so absorbed in something you were doing for fun that you entered into what's best described as a state of flow, where it seems like time slows down and your thoughts shift into a different gear. That state brings you into the moment; you aren't worrying about what's to come or rehashing the past. It's mindfulness, which is simply paying attention to what's happening right now, without judgment. The more time you spend in this mental zone, the more clearly you think and the happier you are.

I have a client named Susan who was nearly dead when we met, she was so debilitated by her second round of chemo. She had been smoking two packs of cigarettes, drinking two extra-large Dunkin Donuts coffees a day, and eating fast food all the time because she was so stressed out from work, and she was just trying to keep going. We worked together for a few months, and now Susan prioritizes doing things that make her happy. She putters around the house working on little home improvement projects. She cooks dinner for her two daughters. She's in such a happy place in her mind that it has prevented her cancer from coming back. The doctors don't understand why she's still in remission, as most often this type of cancer does return, but her tumors aren't growing.

I share this story with you because I want you to know that no matter where you're starting from, you can find the time, and you can reap the benefits of spending time in the creative zone.

We all have creative energy—it emanates out of the second chakra, which is located in your pelvis (it's also where your sexual energy originates)—and everyone's creative energy is unique. This creativity needs expression or else the second chakra can become blocked, preventing energy from flowing freely throughout the rest of the body, including through the heart. It's good for your heart to see and appreciate the things that you have created, and appreciate yourself for making them; it's gratifying to make something that didn't exist before, and that gratification feeds your heart.

The only catch is that the hobby you pursue should be something that you truly love. Whether you love needlepoint or working on your Harley, when you spend time doing that thing, your heart is generating positive energy that uplifts your whole being. On the other hand, if you're taking up crafting because that's what your friends like to do, or trying to knit something really complicated because you saw it on Pinterest, but it's only frustrating you, it's not really a worthy expenditure of your time and energy. Whatever you decide to do, promise me that it will be something that you truly enjoy. Even if it doesn't make sense to other people.

I have one client who has a whole room set up for painting and sculpting, that's her outlet. For me, I like to read things that are enlightening. I try to read a little every day. While I've been working on this book, writing has been my creative outlet. Once this book is complete,

I look forward to taking on some decorating projects, painting, and making pottery.

If you aren't sure what to do, ask yourself what you enjoyed doing when you were a kid, adolescent, or young adult. Or, more recently, before you were married or before you had kids. You may have to think back a few (or several) years to get some inspiration. There could be something you've been wanting to do more recently, but just haven't found the time for (or given yourself the permission to spend the time on). Things you've never tried before are just as valid as things you have a track record of doing in the past.

The hardest part of doing more of what you enjoy is finding the time. I promise you, the time is there if you allow yourself to see it, just as the time is there for you to exercise and prepare healthier foods. I hope that knowing just how healing hobbies can be will embolden you to carve some time out of your schedule to work on them.

Set Healthy Limits and Boundaries with Your Family

Ninety-nine percent of the hundreds and hundreds of clients I've worked with over the last twenty years have had some kind of issue with their family relationships. For women especially, it is very common to have never set any sort of boundaries with their family members. This leads to unmanaged expectations that typically lead to my clients feeling unappreciated and overburdened by their family members. Worse yet, because it is family we're talking about, it's all too easy to feel like there is nothing that you can do to make things better for yourself. But that simply isn't true.

The first step in improving any problematic relationship is to simply observe it. There's a line in every relationship that can be very hard to see—especially because it is obscured by love, and by the expectations of your family and of society at large. When that line is crossed, it leads to an enabling situation. Enabling is the psychological term for overhelping, and it typically means that you are preventing someone else from taking responsibility and having agency over their own lives. The problem is, it's very hard to detect when you, or someone you're in relationship with, has slipped into enabling because you're so invested in the relationship and the history goes back so far. After all, you want to help them and make them feel better. But nothing you can do is going to make someone else feel 100 percent better. As smart and capable as you are, you can't fix their life for them—that's their job.

To understand what enabling is, imagine that your husband is an alcoholic. You love your husband and you want him to be in a good mood, and because you don't want you or anyone else in your family to be vulnerable to his rages if he doesn't have enough alcohol, you make sure you pick up some booze for him on your way home from work every day. In this way, you become his enabler; he relies on you to regulate his mood. Taking care of his need for alcohol makes you feel good because you know you are protecting the household.

Enablers are typically, at their heart, sweet and compassionate. They truly want to help. But enabling has its own risks.

Think of the hypothetical scenario I just mentioned. By buying your husband's liquor every day, you are making it possible for him to live as an alcoholic. You are now responsible for supporting this person you love in a habit that is self-destructive and can cause harm to others.

If you stopped buying the booze, he'd probably have a tantrum. He'd probably then go buy it himself. Maybe he would have a moment of clarity when he sees how much money and effort goes into supporting his addiction, or maybe not. Either way, it takes you out the equation. You are no longer complicit in his dysfunction.

This example is a bit dramatic. I want you to clearly see how enabling works, and how it often comes from a place of good intention. Maybe the person in your family whom you enable is your parent, sibling, or child. Maybe the way you enable them is to always take their calls and listen for hours as they complain. Or you do every errand for them. Or you take them to every doctor's appointment, to the point that you barely have time to take care of your own work, life, and health.

It may feel like you don't have a choice to "overdo" for your relative—this person is your family member, after all. Maybe there's no one else in the family to help. Yet if you never nudge them to take care of themselves, they'll never learn how to do it. When you say, "I can't do this for you anymore," that person will either have to find someone else to over rely on, or they can grow and become more self-sufficient.

The only way you can change the behavior of the people you love is to change your own behavior. By doing so, you require them to adapt to a new reality. Adaptability is a hallmark of being alive—humans need challenge to grow and evolve. Think of it this way; by supporting someone in old, unhelpful, toxic patterns, you are contributing to their demise.

I know this is especially hard for women to hear. It was a woman's role to do everything for everyone else for thousands of years—to cook, shop, do laundry, iron, and clean. If you suspect that you have crossed over into enabling in any of your relationships, know that it's a natural reaction to the expectations that have been passed down from woman to woman for generations. It's a survival mechanism. Now it's time to determine if it has crossed over into a pathology.

For example, one of my clients is in her early twenties. She has had medical problems since she was a baby—including severe allergies and frequent illnesses—and now she has a lot of anxiety. Every little bump this young woman has, her mom swoops in and comes rushing to her aid. This may sound like a normal thing to do, but my client is an adult now. She must learn to deal with her life, just as every other adult must do. By inserting herself into every little crisis the daughter has, the mother is stunting my client's growth. It comes from good intentions—to help—but it has negative consequences.

How much you do for other people can be a crutch you rely on to determine your self-worth. Breaking the enabling cycle gives you the opportunity to learn about yourself and what makes you happy.

It's about shifting out of the need to be accepted by others, and moving into accepting yourself and loving yourself as you are. This is how you learn to nurture your own heart instead of depleting it by trying to make others happy.

What Setting Boundaries Looks Like

Drawing better boundaries with your family is an ongoing process. I did a lot of separating from my own family when I moved up to Vermont in my twenties. I didn't know anybody up there. I spent a lot of time on my own, praying, meditating, and connecting to myself. I did so much healing that I finally got to the point where I didn't care what other people thought about me. I wasn't looking for my family's validation and approval anymore, or anyone's for that matter, and that set me free to be true to myself.

Now, almost two decades later, I live a little over an hour from my parents. My mom has been sick with dementia for more than ten years. It's gotten to the point that she has to live in a facility. My dad manages her care, and takes it upon himself to visit her every single day, no matter what. He is a very sweet, loving, and caring man, and his dedication and commitment to my mother is a beautiful thing to witness, especially in today's world. Yet it's clear that the effort exhausts him. I've talked to my dad about setting better boundaries for himself, but he's not one to listen. I try to point out that mom doesn't know whether he's there or not; she doesn't even know what day it is. It's only his tendency to worry that makes him go every day.

One Wednesday, during the midst of moving my business and my house and when my life was completely upside down, my dad called and asked if I could visit Mom that Sunday because he had made plans to go visit our cousins, who live in another state.

I already had plans to visit her that Saturday, and I had also made arrangements to visit an old friend who lives near my parents that day.

I told him I couldn't come down two days in a row. He got his back up. He told me, "Mom comes first."

I reminded him that Mom didn't need to have a visitor every single day—he could take a day off if it was that important to see the rest of the family. It may sound harsh, and of course I want to help my dad, but I had to set a boundary with him. I was crazed with trying to keep up with my regular obligations, while also making two major moves. Making that trip two days in a row would have exhausted me, and I wanted to avoid that at all costs because I didn't want to get sick. If he wants to drive himself to exhaustion because he feels obligated to fulfill this role in a certain way, then that's his choice, but it doesn't also have to be mine.

The thing about setting boundaries with loved ones is that it protects you from over giving, but it also helps the person you're setting the boundaries with. Even if I had gone to spend that Sunday with my mom, it's not going to fix the underlying issue, which is that my dad feels the need to see her every single day. If I draw the line for me, perhaps I'll help inspire him to draw it for himself, too.

Some people will keep asking you to do things for them; it's on you to say when you've had enough. If you never do, you'll always be knocking yourself out to fulfill their needs. You will never feel like what you do is enough, no matter how hard you try. Your resentment will grow. Inevitably, resentment turns into anger. There will be a wedge in your relationship, and it's a terrible irony that the wedge is there because you long to feel close to this person. To top it off, that person will never realize that they are asking too much, and will never learn how to fulfill their own needs. It's a lose-lose proposition with high stakes—your relationship, your health, and your peace of mind are at risk when you don't draw boundaries.

When you say "no more," that person has to pick herself up by her own bootstraps and start to think about her life differently. She is forced to change and to grow. That is a beautiful thing. And it all starts by you drawing the line and saying no.

Evaluate Where You May Be Enabling

Take a look at your relationships and ask yourself:

- How much do I need this person?
- How much do they need me?
- Is this healthy?
- Does spending time with them make me feel good, or does it make me upset?

Look for the instances that cause you to feel badly, and ask yourself where you need to set boundaries so that you are no longer living in that enabling place.

The beautiful irony is that when you cut the cords of enabling, you create space for a truly respectful and loving relationship to take root. It's like cutting a bush down to stubs so that it can thrive in the seasons to come. I know it may not feel this way at first, but you do have the power to change your relationships for the better.

My husband says if it weren't for me, he never would have seen the toxic dynamics that were going on in his family. He needed help to raise his awareness. Because these are long-term, loving relationships, we all need help seeing what's really going on. *Especially* in the relationships that maybe you don't consider to be troublesome. My clients are often surprised to realize how much dysfunction is in their relationship with the parent or sibling to whom they feel closest.

Find Constructive Ways to Express Your Anger

One emotion that often comes up when examining your family relationships is anger—perhaps anger that you have never felt able to express freely. After all, anger gets a bad rap in our culture, particularly for women. A man who raises his voice and shows his ire is praised as forceful and decisive, a woman who does the same is often portrayed as unhinged, hysterical, or a bitch. It's no wonder that so many of us stuff our anger down. The danger is that unexpressed emotions don't go away; they morph into something else.

For example, anxiety and depression are rooted in unexpressed anger. Women are much more prone to both these conditions than men; it's more socially acceptable for us to be worried or sad than it is for us to be angry. And as I've said, depression and anxiety are both common companions to heart disease.

Anger does have an important purpose—it shows you what you care about, and it highlights places where you may need to do some healing. If the way your mother tries to make you feel guilty because you won't take her to the doctor and pick up her groceries for her leaves you feeling angry, it's showing you that you are tired of your time and your needs not being valued. That's pretty important information to have! Because only when you see a problem can you do something about it.

Anger can also be a great motivator. If you are fired up about something, you're more likely to do something about it than if you were only mildly annoyed.

I'm not suggesting that you start yelling at people more, or picking fights—there are many ways to express your anger that few of us are taught. Here are the methods I teach my clients:

- **Give yourself a buffer.** If someone's really triggering you, remove yourself from the situation, even for a minute, before you respond. Go outside and take some deep breaths, go on a run, or even go to the bathroom. You'll come back with a much clearer head, and you'll be able to say your peace without automatically going into a heated argument. This applies whether you're having a conversation in real time, or you've just gotten an upsetting text or email. I know how tempting it is to respond

in the moment, but you will thank yourself for giving yourself a little bit of space to calm down first!
- **Say it in a letter.** If you're still upset about something, even after responding in a more thoughtful way, write a letter to the person you're angry with. This isn't intended to be a letter that you send—you want to give yourself a chance to say what's on your mind and heart in an unedited way so you can give voice to those emotions without escalating the situation. Include in the letter what you're no longer willing to accept, and then draw a line by stating what you're no longer going to do.

  Getting these thoughts and feelings down on paper gets them out of your head, so you no longer have to carry that burden around. After you've written the unedited letter, you can clean it up and send this version if you like. But even if you don't, writing it out will help you feel and express your anger so that you can move on.
- **Give these thoughts a receptacle.** I am a huge proponent of regular journaling. It doesn't have to be formal—this isn't for publication, after all. Just capture your stream of consciousness on what you're feeling in the moment, and then ask yourself what triggered you. Ideally, you'd do this every day; but even if you journal only a few times a week, you can start to see your anger more objectively and get insights that will help you deal with whatever's bothering you. It's kind of like being your own therapist.

Find Your Way to Forgiveness

After you learn to work with your anger more constructively, your stress levels come down and your thinking gets clearer. That's when you can more easily find your way to acceptance—of yourself, others, and your circumstances—that can even lead to the ultimate healer: forgiveness.

Forgiveness is a powerful healer, because carrying around all that hurt, anger, disappointment, and upset puts more stress on your body, causing more anxiety and depression, which negatively impacts your heart health. In fact, studies have found that forgiving others lowers the risk of heart attack,[28] is associated with healthier cholesterol levels,[29] and reduces blood pressure,[30] as well as pain,[31] stress, depression, and anxiety.[32]

Also, when you forgive others, you learn to forgive yourself. When you forgive, you make a conscious choice to acknowledge that nobody is perfect—not even you.

A lot of people think that you have to feel ready to forgive, but it's not an emotional decision; it's a conscious one. That means that forgiveness is a choice.

Here is how I counsel my patients to find their way to forgive someone, whether that's their husband they squabbled with that morning, or their mother who isn't equipped with the tools to provide the kind of nurturing they crave, or themselves for something they've done, said, or decided.

Step one: Reflect on the situation, and notice how the anger or upset is affecting you. This allows you to get some distance and see things more clearly.

Step two: In order to really see the other side of the situation, you have to **empathize** with the other person. What might be going on in their lives that contributed to the problem? Was it an outside circumstance, or could it be something that's been passed down through the generations? Is it a bad behavioral pattern that has never been broken? When you can see the contributing factors, it will be easier to avoid taking the situation personally. Remind yourself that no one is perfect; we all make mistakes, and inevitably, we sometimes hurt each other.

Step three: Apply this same objectivity to yourself. When you let go of trying to be perfect, then you won't have such high standards for others, and you'll be able to better **manage your own expectations**. You will likely become more forgiving of others knowing how unrealistic your expectations truly are.

One last powerful technique for inviting more forgiveness into your heart is to do a loving-kindness prayer. Sitting comfortably in a quiet spot, close your eyes and say the following phrases to yourself:

May I be filled with loving kindness
May I be well
May I be peaceful and at ease
May I be calm and forgive myself and others
Repeat four times.

Next, call up an image of the person you want to forgive in your mind. Then silently repeat the following phrases to yourself:

May she [use her name] be filled with loving kindness
May she [use her name] be well
May she [use her name] be peaceful and at ease
May she [use her name] be calm and forgive herself and others
Repeat four times.

Finally, think about someone you love with all your heart, call up an image of them in your mind's eye, and plug their name into the prayer.

Now you'll know exactly what to do the next time you find yourself carrying anger, resentment, and unforgiveness toward someone—even if that person is you.

CHAPTER 7

THE MISSING LINK FOR TRUE HEART HEALTH

A common thread among the people who find their way to my office is that they feel defined and confined by the roles they play in their lives—their job title, their marital status, whether or not they have kids. They don't know who they are outside of their family and their work. They feel disconnected, aimless, and lost. These feelings are giving them a lot of big-picture angst that causes them to wonder what they're doing with their lives.

I can relate. When I was having my heart troubles, I had spent the last several years racing around trying to do what I was "supposed" to do—go to college, get my master's, get a job at a big company, making money. And because I am a woman, I was expected to be tending to my parents' needs, while also seeking to start a family of my own.

I was knocking myself out in an effort to fulfill my family's and society's expectations. I was so busy trying to achieve what everyone else expected me to do that I stopped paying attention to what I wanted. When I look back on my experiences with heart disease, I see this disconnection from myself as the true crux of the problem. Yes, getting off caffeine helped calm my racing heart. Yes, getting out of a stressful job with a long commute reduced my stress. But what really changed things for me was that I started listening to and trusting my own inner voice. And the thing that helped me do that was fostering my spirituality, which I define as nurturing the connection between you and a higher power, whether you want to call it God, love, the universe, or any other name.

To heal my body, I had to change my outer life and my inner life; I had to discover and accept who I was at my core. I had to remember that I am more than just a member of a family, or a person of a certain profession, or even *just* a human being. I am, just as you and everyone else who has ever lived on this planet are, one-of-a-kind, irreplaceable manifestations of the same force that created the stars, the sky, the Earth, and everything on it. We are more than a body and a brain; we are imbued with a higher intelligence. When we forget this truth, we forget who we truly are. We feel isolated, overburdened, out of our league—maybe even like we are living the wrong life. And we find it very difficult to make the decisions that will ultimately lead us to more peace and fulfillment. We've got to reconnect to this higher intelligence if we want to make the changes that will provide lasting benefit to our heart, our health, and our lives.

Connecting to a Higher Power Helps You Heal

There is a crucial ingredient to true vitality and health that very few healthcare practitioners ever address. And that is your spirituality—a piece that is missing from most people's lives.

I use the word "spirituality" to describe a connection between an individual and a higher power. Without a belief in something bigger than yourself—however you define it—you will tend to get subsumed by meeting external expectations, and to overlook or dismiss the opportunities that magnify who you are at your core.

Sadly, very few of us have an active spiritual life. In our society, the only place spirituality is typically addressed is at church. Many of my patients were raised in a religious tradition that they have since lapsed from. Perhaps you were raised going to church every Sunday, but somewhere along the way you stopped going. Or maybe you go to church regularly, but you aren't getting the sense of connection, faith, and uplift from it that you're craving. Or maybe you never went (and never want to). It doesn't matter what your relationship to religion has been; you can still connect to the universal intelligence, and use it to help you heal.

Even if you don't have a spiritual bone in your body, you still need to establish a connection to the intelligence that infuses every living thing. There is no one right fix that will heal your life and your body, mind, and spirit. Even though I can help you learn the tools and techniques that will support your own healing process, I can't tell you precisely what mix of changes you should make, because your path needs to be customized to you. A spiritual practice that connects you with a higher consciousness can help you more clearly hear what your intuition is telling *you* that you need. And that is a crucial piece of taking your healing into your own hands.

Defining "A Higher Power"

There are many different ways to think of the higher power I'm talking about in this chapter. Of course, different religions call it God (or Yahweh, Jehovah, or Allah). But there are scientific explanations, too. Carl Jung, one of the fathers of modern psychology, believed that every living person is born with access to a universal wisdom called the collective unconscious, and that this connection is a rich source of guidance and inspired thinking that doesn't come from the individual, but from the consciousness that unites us all.

Max Planck, a Nobel Prize-winning physicist, and a contemporary and friend of Albert Einstein, wrote about a force that creates all matter he called "a conscious and intelligent mind." As Planck described it, this force is the matrix of all matter.

More recently, physicists have discovered what's known as a zero-point energy (ZPE) field—an energetic frequency that underlies and gives rise to all matter. In his 2007 book, *Science and the Akashic Records*, philosopher and scientist Ervin Laszlo explains how the ZPE field corresponds to what mystics and sages have long referred to as the Akashic Records, which are believed to be a history of every person, deed, and thought that has ever existed.

I know this may sound pretty "out there," but I find this scientific confirmation of what spiritual teachers have long taught exciting; it shows how much more information and guidance we have access to than what our individual brains can dream up.

Even very practical recovery programs talk about the importance of spirituality. In every twelve-step program, the third step is seeking a higher power to help you overcome your challenges. It's not tacked onto the end as a nice-to-have—it's the third step! Why? Because it's hard to cut through biology, genetics, stress, and the repetition compulsion without help from a higher power.

In order to break free from bad habits, as well as all the external expectations of your family and the culture at large, you need to martial all your resources. The divine intelligence that infuses everything in the universe is the greatest resource there is.

When you develop your connection to your higher power, you feel supported because you no longer have to figure everything out on your own. No matter what challenges you are facing, you are not in this alone—the universe has your back. You also see your unique place in this world, making you less prone to feeling like you have to do what everyone else is doing.

This higher consciousness is always available to you; there's no need to go chasing it. All you have to do is choose to get quiet and listen. It's not hard work. In fact, it's much easier to tap into to the universal intelligence than it is to run around town, visiting ten different doctors. And did I mention, it's free? You can get started right now by using any of the techniques I outline in this chapter.

Each of the practices I am about to introduce will help you open up that spiritual connection. These are tried-and-true techniques that, in many cases, people have been using for thousands of years to access their inner wisdom. But first, I want to introduce you to the part of the brain that makes the opening possible.

Take Care of Your Pineal Gland and It Will Take Care of You

The pineal gland is as big as a pea and shaped like a pine cone; it is located in the very center of your brain, behind the midpoint of your forehead between your eyes. Despite its small size, the pineal gland is one of the most important parts of the nervous system. It works with the hypothalamus to control thirst, hunger, sexual desire, body temperature, and the aging process. Perhaps most importantly, the pineal gland is your connection to higher consciousness. Ancient yogis called it the third eye, French philosopher Rene Descartes called it "the seat of the soul," and Plato referred to it as "the eye of wisdom."

The information that the pineal gland helps you access is like the Force in the *Star Wars* movies. Remember the scene when Luke Skywalker was training to learn how to use his light saber while the blast shield of his helmet covered his eyes? He was learning how to stimulate his pineal gland and develop his inner sight—and you can do it, too.

There are a few ways to open your pineal gland: meditation, prayer, conscious relaxation, and even certain psychedelic drugs (some of which are now being studied by psychologists as a way to cure depression and other mental illnesses). For the sake of this chapter, I'll stick to the legal avenues that you can do on your own, at any time, with no risk. I'll also share with you my favorite relaxation practices. These are the practices my clients love the most, and I hope that you will, too.

Most of the techniques that I'm about to share ask you to keep your attention focused on what is happening in your body for a sustained period of time. This isn't as easy as it might sound; no matter how strong your intentions are to focus on your breathing during meditation, or on different body parts during a body scan, your mind will soon get bored and return to churning out its typical string of thoughts. And that's okay; in fact, it's to be expected, as it takes a long time to change old habits, and your mind has many of them.

Over time, you will feel more comfortable with these practices. But even on the days when you struggle or it feels like you didn't do them "right," you will still be building your focus muscles, unlearning your stressful thinking habits, activating the pineal gland, and firming up your connection to that higher consciousness.

As you embark on these exercises, it helps to remember that they are all an opportunity to practice nonjudgment. So, when you're meditating and you notice that you've started thinking about what to have for dinner, resist the urge to get upset with yourself or to label your thoughts as bad. Just acknowledge the thought that has surfaced, and then go back to focusing on your breathing. You may have to return your attention to your chosen focus 200 times during a ten-minute body scan—you are still reaping huge benefits for yourself in the moment, and planting seeds of healing that will continue to grow and blossom as you keep practicing over time.

Learn How to Let Go with Conscious Relaxation

I like to think of conscious relaxation as a gateway drug to other contemplative practices—my clients and I both find that conscious relaxation is easier than meditation, especially for beginners. And it makes you feel so palpably relaxed that you will naturally want to continue experimenting with other practices, such as meditation.

Conscious relaxation is exactly what it sounds like—using your cognitive powers to produce a relaxed state. The practice builds body awareness, focus, and empowerment—because once you know how to do it, you never need to feel trapped in a stress reaction again.

I'm excited to introduce you to my—and my clients'—favorite conscious relaxation practice: a body scan. This is a process of systematically placing your attention on each and every part of your body and inviting them to relax, one-by-one.

You can do a body scan anywhere, but to really give yourself a treat, set up a special spot in your home that is quiet, clean, and inviting. It will help you relax even further, and seeing that spot all set up and ready to go will help entice you to do this practice more frequently than if you have to clear off a spot on the floor each time.

Body Scan

Time: 20–40 minutes

If you can, practice this three to five days a week for six to eight weeks. Consistency will help you reap the most benefits.

How to Practice

- A body scan can be performed lying down or sitting. Close your eyes if that feels good to you. If not, it's okay to keep them open.
- When you are comfortable, begin by taking a few deep breaths in through your nose and letting them out through your mouth.
- Let your breath return to normal, and then turn your attention to your body, feeling the weight of it on the chair or on the floor. Notice where your body is in contact with the floor or chair, and where it isn't.
- Now place your attention on your feet. Notice the sensations of your feet touching the floor—the weight, pressure, vibration, and temperature. Then imagine every bone, muscle, and cell in your foot releasing any tension.

- Next, notice your legs—is there pressure, pulsing, heaviness, lightness? Then visualize any tightness or tension in your legs disappearing.
- Move your attention up to your back and see what sensations you can feel there. Invite any stress in the muscles and bones of your back to release.
- Now bring your attention into your stomach area. If your stomach is tense or tight, let it go and relax.
- Notice your hands. See if you can allow them to relax.
- Now pay attention to your arms. Feel any sensations happening there. Let your shoulders drop and your muscles release.
- Notice your neck and throat. Let go of tension and tightness. Relax.
- Soften your jaw. Let your face and facial muscles go slack. Let go of any tension and tightness that may be there.
- Then expand your awareness to take in your whole body, feeling how it feels to be in your body, in this moment. Stay here and breathe, savoring how it feels to be right here, right now.
- When you are ready to come out of the relaxed state, rub your hands together to generate heat in your palms, and then place your hands over your eyes for a breath or two.
- Slowly remove your hands, open your eyes, and come back to the room.
- Notice how you feel.
- Thank yourself for providing the space to connect to your mind, body, and spirit.

For a deeper dive into conscious relaxation, try yoga nidra. Also known as yogic sleep, yoga nidra is considered to be more restorative than actual sleep, because of the profound state of rest it creates. The best way to experience yoga nidra is to either take a class in it (check your local yoga studios or centers of natural health) or listen to a guided yoga nidra audio on the internet. I've created one for you and made an audio recording of it available at drsamartano.com and holistichealingmindbodyspirit.com.

Quiet the Mind with Meditation

Meditation is a great way to stimulate the pineal gland and gain access to the wisdom and insight available in the collective unconscious. It also has an impressive list of tangible physical benefits, including:

- Lower levels of stress hormones, including cortisol, and markers of inflammation[33]
- Reduced anxiety[34]
- Long-term decreases in depression[35]
- Fewer feelings of loneliness[36]
- Improved problem-solving[37]
- Increased attention span[38]
- Reducing cravings and emotional eating[39]
- Falling asleep more easily and staying asleep longer[40]
- Less chronic pain[41]
- Lower blood pressure[42]

Despite all these benefits, meditating can be challenging, especially when you are new to it. It's not easy to sit still. It's not easy to tolerate boredom. And it's certainly not easy to ignore your thoughts. That's why I recommend that everyone start out with a meditation practice that is as simple as possible. The following practice is the basic meditation that I teach to all my clients, many of whom have never meditated before.

Basic Meditation

Time: 5–30 minutes, gradually working your way up as you become more comfortable.

There is no one correct length of time to practice meditation. When you first start meditating, aim for 5–10 minutes. As you become more comfortable with your practice, experiment with meditating for longer periods of time.

How to Practice

- Sit on the floor in a cross-legged position with your buttocks resting on a cushion, in a chair, or on a stool. Imagine a thread extending from the top of your head, pulling your spine, neck, and head up toward the ceiling in a straight line.
- Close your eyes and scan your body, relaxing each body part one at a time. Begin with your toes, feet, ankles, shins, and continue moving up until you have relaxed your entire body. Pay special attention to your shoulders, neck, eyes, and jaw, which are common areas for us to hold tension.
- Now that you are sitting tall and have released the tension from your body, be still. There's nowhere to go and nothing to do—allow yourself to enjoy this brief vacation from "doing."
- Turn your attention to your breath. Notice how it feels in your nose, throat, chest, and belly as it flows in and out. Engage your diaphragm to fill your lungs, but do not force your breath.
- If you'd like something a little more tangible to focus on, choose to silently repeat a mantra. A mantra is a sound, word, or phrase that you repeat silently throughout your meditation session. A simple mantra for beginners is to say, "I am breathing in" with each inhale and "I am breathing out" with each exhale.
- As you focus on your breath or your mantra, thoughts will continue to come into your mind. When they do, simply acknowledge them, set them aside, and return your attention to your breath or mantra.
- When you are ready to end your practice, slowly bring your attention back to your surroundings. Gently wiggle your fingers and toes. Begin to move your hands, feet, arms, and legs. Then open your eyes. Move slowly and take your time getting up.

When it comes to meditation, consistency is more important than quantity. Meditating for five minutes every day will reward you with far greater benefits than meditating for two hours once a week.

Change Your Reality with Affirmations

This next practice that I'm about to share with you comes from metaphysics—the scientific discipline where I earned my PhD; it is the study of the nature of reality. According to metaphysics, everything in the universe—whether it's something solid, like a building, or something intangible, like an emotion or a thought—is made of energy. And the way this energy moves and communicates is through vibration. Every person, thing, circumstance, thought, and emotion has a particular vibration, or frequency. When it comes to energy, like attracts like. Something with an energy that is low vibration will attract something else at a similar frequency, like a magnet to metal.

While metaphysics may seem very theoretical, with no bearing on your life, it actually is very practical after you know how to work with it. Because like attracts like, when you raise your vibration, you get results that match this raised frequency.

From a religious perspective, metaphysics is basically the scientific version of karma and the Golden Rule—what you put out, you get back.

This isn't just woo-woo, *The Secret*-type stuff. The study of metaphysics is built on the foundation of Einstein's discovery of the quantum-sized fields of radiation emitted from every particle. Nobel Prize–winning physicist Richard Feynman discovered that the electrons in our brains can be activated by these quantum waves. As Candace Pert wrote about in her book *Molecules of Emotion*, everything you think and feel has a vibration associated with it. If you want a higher vibration, you simply have to raise the frequency of your thoughts and feelings.

My favorite way to do just that is to use affirmations—positive statements that you repeat silently to yourself. Saying affirmations creates new neural pathways, cues the release of feel-good neurochemicals, and crowds out negative thoughts. The more you repeat them, the more you raise the frequency of your emotions and your energy, which helps to draw more desirable outcomes and opportunities to you.

Affirmations

Time: Anywhere from 30 seconds to 30 minutes

It's nice to repeat affirmations to yourself as you are sitting quietly, either before or after your body scan or meditation. Being in a relaxed state will help the meaning of the affirmations penetrate more deeply into your consciousness. But you certainly don't have to limit yourself to that. You can repeat affirmations hundreds of time a day with every step you take, while you're on hold waiting for the conference call to start, or as you chop the vegetables for dinner. The more you do, the more you're going to raise your frequency, and the more you'll attract new things into your life that make your heart sing.

How to Practice

- Decide how long you'll practice your affirmations first. Then repeat the following four sentences to yourself silently for your chosen duration:

   I love myself.
   I accept myself.
   I approve of myself.
   I forgive myself.

If that is too much to remember, you can start off by simply repeating to yourself, *I love myself,* then gradually work your way up to saying all four.

- If you are prone to worry and anxiety, start off with these affirmations:

   I am calm.
   I am at peace.

Once you are feeling more relaxed, you can begin to repeat the group of affirmations that starts with *I love myself.*

A Long-Term Practice for Long-Term Results

One of my clients, Marie, suffers from depression. She and I have been working together for over a year, discussing constructive ways for her to express her feelings to her loved ones, and to be more assertive with coworkers and friends. All during the time we've worked together, Marie has regularly come to my yoga class. She would always say how great it made her feel—how relaxed and at ease in her body. She would admit, though, that she didn't really get what I meant when I would talk about connecting to a higher consciousness. Still, she kept coming to class.

Then, in one of our recent sessions, Marie walked into the room with tears in her eyes. I asked her what was wrong. She said; "Nothing is wrong at all, in fact, everything feels so right!"

Marie had been in my yoga class the night before, and during one of the poses where I talked my students through imagining a ball of energy traveling up and down their body, something shifted for her. "I felt a connection to something greater than me. It felt beautiful, amazing. A sense of peace came over me. I feel like I finally got it—how to connect the mind to the body, let go, and let God in," she said.

I got goose bumps, knowing that she had learned how to access her own divine guidance. Since then, Marie has been feeling more like she just *knows* how to interact more authentically and stick up for herself with the people in her life—she hasn't had to think so much about *how* to do it. "I don't know how to explain it, exactly, but I feel stronger and more whole. The funny thing is that this feeling comes from quieting my mind and being still. Now I see that when I give myself this time to get quiet, answers come to me easily."

It's such an important and powerful moment, when you get that spiritual connection. It rarely comes instantaneously, however. As with Marie, it can take a few months or even a year, or more, before you have an aha moment, and that is totally okay. After all, eternal wisdom has a different relationship to time than we do. So just know that in order to be truly transformative, you need to do these practices over the long-term.

That may sound like a tall order, but the good news is that each time you practice conscious relaxation, meditation, or affirmations, you will love the sensation of quieting your mind and feeling present. You will appreciate it so much, in fact, that you will be compelled to do your practice again the next day (or as soon as you can). Each time, you'll build a stronger connection to the higher consciousness that will deliver profound benefits to your body, your life, and your healing process.

CHAPTER 8

FINE-TUNE YOUR PROGRAM

When my client, Stephanie, returned to my office again (we had worked together many years ago), she had a long list of troubling concerns. As a single mom of two young girls, with a high-stress job and long commute, Stephanie was suffering from frequent anxiety. It had gotten so bad that she had started getting panic attacks, and had recently fainted at work. Stephanie also had diverticulitis (an inflammation of the GI tract) and had gained twenty pounds since we first worked together. She also frequently experienced heart palpitations and was on high blood pressure medication. Basically, she was on track for a heart attack.

When Stephanie went to see her doctor about the fainting spell, he recommended that she see a therapist. Because we had already worked together, she knew right away that she wanted to come see me.

After Stephanie got me up to speed on her health challenges, we talked about her goals for treatment, including not just the "what," but the "why." In the short-term, Stephanie wanted to reduce her panic and anxiety, and alleviate the diverticulitis so that she felt better on a daily basis. Over the longer term, she wanted to lose weight, dramatically lower her stress levels, and improve her heart health. When I asked her why these things were important to her, Stephanie said that what she wanted more than anything else was to be around for her children well into their adulthood. Her recent health scares had forced her to contemplate the fact that she might not live into old age.

After Stephanie had named her objectives, we developed a treatment plan that addressed her health challenges, while also honoring the realities of her life and her busy schedule.

The first change Stephanie implemented was to start taking twenty-minute walks to clear her head and move her body. She started off doing one walk during the week (between meetings or on her lunch break), and once on the weekends.

Because her diverticulitis was causing her a lot of discomfort, we also worked on removing foods from her diet that aggravated her condition. Those changes, along with her walks, helped her start losing weight pretty quickly.

Next, we worked on Stephanie weaning herself off coffee, something she relied on to keep her energy up throughout the day. I explained that the stimulation coffee provided may make her feel like she could work harder, but it was also contributing to her heart palpitations, as well as her overall sense of anxiousness. I encouraged her to drink peppermint tea instead. Not only does it taste delicious and have a refreshing scent, it is also a digestive aid that could soothe her stomach. This change was harder for Stephanie to implement because coffee was more than a beverage to her. It was a lifestyle. While she started drinking one cup of peppermint tea a day right away—and immediately noticed that it helped her stomach feel better—she also kept drinking her coffee for a good six months before she was fully ready to cut the cord.

Stephanie also started coming to my yoga classes religiously, which helped her get into that relaxed state where healing can happen. She decided to think differently about two things she was already doing—cooking and spending time with her girls. She began to think of these two activities as hobbies instead of obligations. This wasn't so much of a change in behavior, as a change in mindset that helped Stephanie see these daily activities as an opportunity to nourish her creative side.

Now, a year later, Stephanie has lost all of those twenty pounds. She's come off her high blood pressure medication, and her anxiety and panic levels are practically nonexistent. She says she feels amazing, and her doctor is also impressed with her progress. Better yet, Stephanie knows that she feels better as a direct result of the changes she's worked to make. That gratification makes her successes all the sweeter.

These are the kinds of changes that are possible for you, too, when you develop a personalized plan that addresses your specific challenges. In this chapter, you'll learn how to do just that.

The Power of Starting Slowly

In all the chapters leading up to this point, I've shared many strategies that I and my clients have used to create major improvements in our heart health. The only problem is that sometimes having a lot of options can be paralyzing. On top of that, changing long-standing behaviors can feel like a mountain that's just too big to climb.

The great news is that healing isn't a rush job; it takes time. How is that good news? It means you don't have to do it all in a day, or even a month. All you need to do is start small. Making even a few tiny tweaks to your normal routine—you start getting to yoga class once a week, and you wean yourself off the foods that don't agree with your body—will kick off an upward spiral. Those simple adjustments will give you a little more energy and help you build momentum. That will make it easier to take the next step and find time to meditate. Then, spending time quieting your mind will help give you the clarity and the resilience you need to draw better boundaries with your family. In this way, one positive change makes the next one easier to do.

There's a scientific reason why ramping up gradually is a smart strategy. When you achieve a small goal, it releases dopamine—a neurotransmitter that lights up the reward center of the brain and gives a pleasurable feeling. That dose of dopamine will help train you to keep doing the things that create that pleasant sensation. In the meantime, it will also help you feel happier.

It's like getting back to the gym after a long time away. Better to do a light workout that makes you feel strong and energized, and raring to do it again, than to go in and lift so much weight that you can't walk for a week and never go back. Steady wins the race!

To Get Where You Want to Go, You Need a Plan

Setting goals for yourself is something that will help organize your thoughts, and start doing the things that will make you happier in the short-term, while transforming your health over the long-term. Goals take your good ideas and turn them into a plan. They help you customize your plan to your exact needs, wants, realities, and likes. And they keep you on track.

Without tangible, specific, and doable goals, you'll forget what you're working toward and why it matters to you. When that happens, it will be all too easy to talk yourself out of doing the things that will lead to the positive changes you're seeking. You'll tell yourself you're too busy, it's too hard, or you were crazy to think you could make this change in the first place. And you absolutely deserve to feel accomplished and excited about your health and your life.

How to Set Goals that Work

Goal-setting is a skill—one that rarely comes naturally and isn't often taught in schools. That's a real shame, because having goals makes you significantly more likely to be successful.

Researchers have discovered many elements of successful goals. One of my favorite experiments was conducted by Dr. Gail Matthews, a psychology professor at Dominican University of California. In this study, 267 people were asked to set goals. Group one was told to only think about their goals. Group two was asked to think about and then write those goals down. Group three was asked to do the same as Group two, with the addition of writing down their commitment to taking action toward their goal. Group four did the same as Group three, as well as telling a friend about their goals. And Group five did the same as Group four—their extra assignment was to send a weekly progress report to their friend.

At the end of the four-week study period, 43 percent of Group one either achieved their goal or were more than halfway there, compared to 62 percent of Group four. And a whopping 76 percent of Group five met their goals.

This research shows how important it is to write your goals down, commit to a plan of action, and, if at all possible, have an accountability partner. Before we start determining which goals you want to commit to, there's one step that's vital to take so that you ensure that your goals will actually get you where you want to go, and that's determining what your big-picture objectives are first.

Objectives Plot Your Course

You wouldn't set out on a road trip without deciding your final destination, otherwise, who knows where you might end up. The same is true for goal-setting—you want to know where you want your efforts to take you. That's where objectives come in.

Objectives are the big-picture things you are seeking to create; a more fulfilling work situation, feeling more supported in your relationships, or an abiding sense of vitality and peace are all examples of objectives. Goals are the measurable, finite endeavors that make your objectives a reality.

Here are some examples that demonstrate the difference:

Objective	Goals
Financial freedom	Paying off credit card debt
	Saving $1,000 in an emergency fund
	Earning more money
Improving relationship with your mother	Setting better boundaries
	Practicing loving-kindness
	Meditating regularly
	Finding an activity you can enjoy together

Objective	Goals
Feeling great in your body	Establishing a regular yoga practice
	Removing foods that don't agree with you
	Walking three times a week
Being around in twenty years to see grandkids graduate from college	Eating a healthier diet
	Meditating or doing yoga regularly to Reducing stress
	Exercising at least three times a week

To begin naming your objectives, ask yourself:

- What do I want to create more of in my life that will help me in these areas?

Notice that I worded the question above as what you want *more* of, not what you want *less* of. This is an important distinction; you want to write your objectives in a way that is positive, not negative. Instead of saying you want less stress, say you want to feel more at peace.

Wanting less stress in your life, for example, is a perfectly fine objective. However, if you word it that way, you put too much emphasis on what you *don't* want, which is stress. As I covered in Chapter 7, our thoughts and feelings emit a frequency that attracts things that match the same frequency. So, if you focus on having less stress, you'll be subconsciously drawing stressful situations to you. But when you make it your objective to feel more at peace, you emit an energetic frequency that helps draw things to you that create more peace in your life. How you say what you want matters.

After you've thought about what you want more of in your life, write all your answers down in a list. Then see if you can consolidate those answers into a list of three to five objectives. Don't worry yet about how you'll make them happen, we'll get to that in just a moment. Right now, anything is on the table. Go ahead and do it. I'll wait. (There's a blank page at the end of this chapter where you can record your objectives, if you like.)

Set Goals that Support Your Objectives

Your next step is to take each objective, and make a list of goals that will help make that big idea a reality. In my practice, I set goals for every client that consist of three parts:

- **Subject.** Your goal has to have a main idea—the *what* that you are committing to doing. That main idea needs to be specific, doable, and relevant to helping you get what *you* want (and not something you think you should be doing because someone else is doing it). Instead of "eat better," say; "eat at least one serving of vegetables at every lunch and dinner." That's specific, doable, and relevant. It will probably be challenging to really be that specific, and to keep your goal within the realm of possibility. We tend to think we have to completely change everything about our life to make meaningful progress. I'm willing to bet you'll have to make a couple of tries at writing your goals in this way, and that is okay. Revise them as many times as you need, in order to get them to a place where you feel confident that you can actually achieve them.
- **Date.** For each goal that you set, write down when you want to have achieved it by. This can feel a little risky, or arbitrary, but do it anyway. Setting a deadline for yourself creates a sense of urgency, which will help keep you motivated. Just be sure to check your expectations—if you have a goal of paying off $10,000 in debt, you probably won't be able to do that in a month (no matter how much you would love to complete it that quickly). Or if you

are clinically depressed, you may not be able to lose ten pounds in three months, because at first it will be enough of an achievement just to get out of bed. Be realistic about where you are and what's doable for you. With my clients, we often give each goal a timeline of six months—it's not too far away, and not too soon, either. It allows for you to get off track during a busy period and still have time to recover, but it's not so long from now that you can justify blowing it off.

Setting a date also helps you prioritize your goals. If you want to have a new job by a year from now, but want to be exercising regularly in three months, you'll know that you need to focus on exercise first. When you've gotten to the point where you are exercising more with a lot of extra effort, you can focus more on your job search.

One thing setting a date shouldn't do is stress you out. If it's been six months and you're still working on a particular goal, it's okay. What matters is that you are taking consistent steps and making regular progress.

- **Frequency.** This is how often you'll work on your goal. Whenever possible, say how often you'll do the main idea of your goal. Remember to start slowly; you can work your way up over time.

Now take a moment to write out a clear list of your goals for the next six months. Again, I've included a blank goal-setting worksheet at the end of this chapter that you can use if you like. Wherever you record your goals, be sure to keep it in a place that is easily accessible.

If you need ideas for what goals to include on your list, I've compiled a list to help refresh your memory. I'm including a list of all the strategies we've covered this far in the book. You don't have to put *all* of these on your list of goals—I just want you to be able to see at a glance the choices available to you. You can also add in other goals that are more personal to you. After all, this plan has to work for *you*.

Strategies for Supporting Heart Health

Prioritizing Your Emotional Health

- Create a genogram to see the behaviors and thoughts you may have inherited
- Journal regularly to get all your feelings out of your head and off your chest
- Write a letter to someone you're angry with (you don't have to send it, remember, you're just giving voice to your feelings)
- Research a mental health counselor if that feels like a good fit for you

Improving Your Diet

- Avoid inflammatory foods
- Upgrade your fats
- Eat less meat (and upgrade the meat you do eat)
- Remove foods that are aggravating to you
- Reduce dependency on caffeine, alcohol, and sugar
- Find an eating program to follow
- Reduce emotional eating
- Say thanks before you eat

Moving Your Body More

- Aim for twenty minutes of aerobic exercise, such as walking, three times a week; start slow and work your way up
- Stretch at least three times a week
- Do some kind of strength training twice a week
- Or, hit all these categories by practicing yoga; work your way up to doing it four times a week, whether in a class or on your own
- Do a breathing practice one to two times a week (can be part of your yoga practice)

Make Your Work More Fulfilling

- Find ways to make your current job or work situation more meaningful
- If that's not possible, start exploring options for a new job by taking small steps—updating your LinkedIn profile, getting your resume together, etc.

Spend More Time Doing What You Love

- Decide on a hobby you'd like to pursue or re-prioritize
- Set a schedule for spending time on this hobby

Improve Your Family Relationships

- Draw better boundaries; practice saying "no" with love
- Experiment with new ways to deal with situations that make you angry
- Find your way to forgiveness for those who have hurt you
- Practice loving-kindness meditation

Grow Your Connection to a Higher Power

- Practice conscious relaxation with a body scan or yoga nidra
- Start meditating
- Use affirmations to create more feelings of peace

Remember to Follow Your Heart

Throughout this process of naming your objectives and setting your goals, let your heart lead the way instead of your head. Your mind may tell you to be practical and make your objective to get a promotion at your current company, which you can't stand, while your heart votes for looking for a job at a company with a mission that resonates with you. Your head may be repeating the voice of a doctor who is telling you that you're only option is to try another surgery, or be on medication for the rest of your life, while your heart maintains that what you really need is to reduce your stress.

Women are so programmed to put our wants and needs after those of others. Let this process be where you put yourself—and your heart—first. To give your heart a say in this process, use one of the techniques I covered in Chapter 7—such as meditating or doing a body scan—before you sit down to write out your objectives and goals.

Put Your Goals into Action

Now that you have your goals written down and have given yourself deadlines for achieving them, it's time to develop and commit to an action plan.

Looking at your list of goals, ask yourself which goal is most doable, which is the most urgent, and which will have the biggest impact on your well-being. These are the goals you want to focus on first. (They may not be three separate goals—if one goal meets two or all these criteria, start with that one.)

Then get out your calendar and look at when you can find the time to work on them. I counsel my clients to schedule their yoga class, or their twenty-minute walk, or their ten minutes of meditation just as they would any other meeting. That way, you'll be careful not to overschedule yourself. If you use an electronic calendar, you'll also likely get a nice automatic reminder to do the thing that serves your goal. You may feel that you don't have the time for these pursuits, but I promise you, the time is there. You simply have to look for it, and then protect it. This is a crucial step in integrating your goals into your life.

You can always re-work your plan and find a different time if your original schedule doesn't work out, but you have to start somewhere. It may take you a few weeks to actually get to that first yoga class, and that is okay. So long as you keep it on your calendar and keep reminding yourself that this is something you want to do, you *will* get there.

Using an Accountability Partner to Stay Motivated

One final piece of effective goal-setting is accountability. Remember how in the study I mentioned at the start of this chapter, the group that regularly updated a friend on their progress had the highest success rate in meeting their goals? To give yourself your highest probability of success, you want to at least tell someone you trust about the changes you're seeking to make. Ideally, you'd also commit to giving this person regular updates about your progress.

One of the nice things about meeting with a mental health counselor or other professional regularly is that you know you're going to have some built-in accountability. In every session I have with my clients, we review their goals and I ask them how many times they've exercised, how their dietary changes are going, how much time they've spent on their hobbies, and for specifics about whatever else is on their particular list of treatment goals.

It really doesn't matter who your accountability partner is, so long as you can trust them to be nonjudgmental, and to care enough to keep checking in with you. It can be a great way to deepen your relationship, too.

Keeping Yourself on Track

An important tactic to help you stay motivated after the initial excitement about making changes has passed is one that most people miss: re-reading your goals on a regular basis. After all, if you write out your goals and stick them in a drawer and never look at them again, you're likely to forget what they were.

That's why I advise you to find a regular time each week to take out your goals and re-read them. It will help you stay mindful of what you're working on, give you a chance to see how much progress you've made, and assess how much time you have left before you want to have achieved this goal. Re-reading your list takes only ten minutes. I find it's a nice thing to do on Monday morning when I'm gearing up for the week. Other good times are Sunday afternoons, when perhaps you have a little extra quiet time, or Friday afternoons; you can see how well you did on taking action toward your goals for that week, and adjust your schedule for the following week if you need to make any tweaks.

This check-in time is also a great opportunity to take a moment to observe how the actions you've been taking are impacting you. Have you lost weight? Are you feeling less anxious? Are you sleeping better? Did you manage to respond more thoughtfully to someone in your family who usually pushes your buttons? When you take time to notice the benefits you're creating for yourself, you'll be more likely to keep doing the things that are creating them.

Stay in It for the Long Haul

A lot of times we think of achieving a goal as an ending point, when really it's just the beginning of a new goal. The truth is, working on your goals is your life's work. It's a daily (or nearly daily) practice. You're never going to get to a point where you don't need to be taking good care of yourself. After all, you don't want to go back to where you were, do you?

The good thing about having a practice is that it's not about being perfect. When you miss a day, you just get back to it the next day. There are no demerits. If you don't view your treatment plan as something you have to do flawlessly, you'll be able to forgive yourself occasional lapses, which makes it much more likely that you'll keep going.

Write Out Your Objectives and Goals Here

<u>Objectives:</u>

- _____
- _____
- _____
- _____

<u>Goals (with deadlines):</u>

- _____
- _____
- _____
- _____
- _____
- _____

<u>The person (people) I'll ask to be my accountability partner is (are):</u>

- _____
- _____
- _____

<u>The day(s) of the week when I'll review my goals is:</u>

_____ and _____

CHAPTER 9

TRUST THE HEALING PROCESS

By this point, I hope that you've taken the time to sit down and write out your objectives, as well as the goals that will help those objectives come true. Now comes the most important part of your treatment plan: to actually follow it, and to keep going.

Your health is always the result of the choices you've made in the days, weeks, months, and even years that have come before this moment. For that reason, the things you do today are the biggest predictors of your future health. Whatever changes you hope to create, in order to maintain them, you will need to keep taking the steps that support those changes. So long as you are alive, there really is no end point to your healing plan. As you meet each objective and goal, you'll simply need to make new ones.

While plans can get derailed by all kinds of good reasons—someone you love gets sick, or you experience a big transition such as a move or the birth of a child—the most common reason I see for women not sticking with their treatment plans is that they stop believing that their efforts are making a difference. That's why the *most important* thing you can do to improve your health on your own is to trust the healing process. Without this trust, you'll start saying things to yourself like, "What's the point?" and, "Oh, it doesn't really matter if I don't do this stuff." With all the distractions and obligations we face every day, if you don't believe that the steps you are taking matter, it will be too easy to blow them off.

The tricky part is that trust takes time to build. As you stick with your program and start seeing how good the changes you're implementing are making you feel, your trust in your own ability to heal will grow naturally. But there may be a gap in time between when you decide to embark on your healing plan, and when you start to notice the benefits. It's during this time that trust matters the most. Without it, you'll be too likely to succumb to doubt and quit.

To help steer you through those early days, think about the changes you are seeking to make in the same way as planting a seed. To help a seed grow to its fullest, you have to prepare the soil, dig the hole, and keep the seed watered and well lit. You can't just pop it into the ground and have a visible plant the next day, or even the next week. There is a period of time when that seed is underground, and even though it is growing, you have no visible evidence that it is there. You simply trust that you will see that baby plant poke its head up through the soil at just the right time.

It's the same with your healing. When you do the things that support your well-being, even though you can't see the progress, change is happening beneath the surface.

It's important to note that while a seed is growing, it isn't methodically checking off a to-do list, or stressing that it hasn't done enough growing yet. It is just doing what it is normally programmed to do. Just as a seed innately knows how to grow, so do you. Within the course of a year, each one of your 75 trillion cells rebuilds itself. That means you effortlessly evolve into a brand new human being each year. So please, resist the urge to try harder. Aim to struggle less, and trust more.

Own Your Responsibilities; Let Go of the Rest

Taking ownership of your own heart health is a big step; it requires you to assume ownership of your present and your future. It can be tempting to interpret this step as putting a lot of new weight on your shoulders. But you don't bear all the responsibility—your body and your inner wisdom are doing a lot of work on your behalf. To keep the healing process from being overwhelming, it helps to be very clear about what is your job, and what isn't.

Here are the things that are on your plate:

- **Staying focused on your goals.** As I said in the previous chapter, you not only want to write down your goals, you also want to re-read them regularly so that you stay present to what's important to you and the changes you're seeking to make. Even if there are weeks where you completely fall off the wagon and don't do any of the things that support your goals, make sure you at least read them over; it will help your mind stay in the game, which means you'll be able to get back on track as soon as you are able.
- **Taking the actions that lead to your goals.** You do actually have to do the work—get to the yoga class, sit in meditation, write in your journal, buy and prepare the healthier foods. There's no way around this. The good news is, the more consistent you are, the more positive benefits you'll create, and the less these actions will feel like work.
- **Forgiving yourself when you miss a day or make a choice you later regret.** It will happen. After all, you're human, and humans are imperfect! If you eat the bag of Jax, or sleep through your early morning workout, or fall back out of the habit of doing your hobby, resist the urge to beat yourself up. Say a simple loving-kindness mantra to yourself, such as; "I forgive myself. I love myself. I take care of myself." And then get back to it. You wouldn't yell at a seed for not growing one day, would you? Show yourself the same patience and compassion.
- **Staying in contact with people who support you.** You are not in this alone. There are people in your life who love you and want the best for you, and will support you in your new choices and behaviors. They may be people you know in the real world—a sibling, friend, co-worker—or they may be someone you find in an online community, like a Facebook group of local moms, or a LinkedIn group for women in your profession. They may be a friend or family member, or they may be a professional whom

you pay for their objective guidance and accountability. Having people who can ask how you are doing, and who listen when you want to share a success, or get help with a challenge, will help you stay on the path and go farther in your journey.

Here's what's not on your to-do list:

- ***Doing* the actual healing.** You are creating the conditions for your body to heal, but your body is doing the healing. You don't have to micromanage this. Do your part, and then let your innate intelligence do the rest. I know delegating doesn't come naturally to a lot of women, but in this instance, you are going to have to outsource most of the actual work to your cells.
- **Managing your body's timeframe.** We are used to taking an ibuprofen pill and feeling our pain recede just a few minutes later. Natural healing takes time. So does Western medicine, if you really think about it—making appointments, waiting for appointments to happen, sitting in the waiting room, scheduling any procedures, waiting to see how your new prescription affects you, recovering from procedures... it all takes time, too. No healing happens on a timetable. The more you can trust in the process, the more you'll also build your patience muscles. If it takes three months instead of two weeks to see your blood pressure come down, and notice that your palpitations have gotten much better, that's okay. The important thing is that it happens at all, not that it happens quickly.

    The body needs the time that it needs. Putting an expectation on yourself for a specific timeframe is stressful, which is counterproductive to healing. As I've said, a typical timeline is six months to change habits and see clear evidence of positive change, but there is no hard and fast rule. Your body is in charge.

- **Overanalyzing or over researching.** Spending too much of your time obsessing over your health—researching online, attending summits, reading only health-related books—is stressful. It overstimulates the sympathetic nervous system, and that will slow down or even stall the healing process. If you know that you tend to overthink, consider working with a professional, whether that's a mental health counselor, a traditional doctor you trust, a nutritionist, an osteopath, an acupuncturist, or another type of practitioner to help you determine your priorities and keep an eye on your progress.

Any time you start to feel overwhelmed, read over this list of what's your responsibility and what's not, and look for ways you might be taking on more of the load than is truly yours to bear.

Listen to Your Body

A key to establishing trust in your ability to heal is to listen to your body. After all, your body is more than just your home; it's also your partner. That means it's not something to be ignored or dragged around. It's something to treat with kindness and respect. That includes listening to the information it provides, and doing what it is asking you to do.

Your body is speaking to you all the time; it's a key component of your inner voice. Yes, sometimes that inner voice will speak in actual words when you've quieted your mind, but sometimes it will be more physical—like a leaden feeling in your stomach, or a heaviness in your heart, or a yearning to sleep.

Of course, you have to be receptive enough to notice what your body is telling you in the first place. When you receive the message, your next step is to honor it. That means that when you notice that you feel tired, you trust yourself enough to do less. Maybe that means going to bed earlier, canceling plans, or allowing yourself to spend the weekend in bed. I can't promise that it's always easy to act on this information your body sends. Your friends may encourage you to come out anyway. Your family may look at you like you're crazy if you say you're not getting out of bed until Monday. But it's your inner voice that you need to put your faith into in these moments—not the opinions of your friends and family. Giving your body the rest it needs, when it needs it, is how you'll repair and restore yourself.

Being able to listen to your body and trust what it's telling you is a process—like any relationship, it needs to build over time. But the more you demonstrate to your body that you're listening, the more in tune you'll be.

Monitor Your Progress

This trust I'm asking you to develop isn't simply blind faith; it's bolstered by keeping an eye on specific components of your overall wellness, so that you can assess the impact of your efforts.

To help you get more clarity on the feedback your body is giving you, I've developed a simple worksheet that cues you to check-in on how you are feeling. Using it regularly will cue you to pause long enough to notice how you're feeling. It will also help you see how your internal sensations are improving over time.

Either in this book, in a notebook, or in a document on your computer, keep a record of how well you feel in the following categories. I recommend checking in on these and recording your answers once a week for at least six months. That way you'll be able to see the trends over time, and won't put too much stock into one particular day. For each category, give yourself a ranking of 1–10, with 1 being the lowest and 10 being the highest. In some categories, like sleep, 10 will be the best rating you can give yourself. But in others, like anxiety, a 10 would mean your anxiety levels are the highest they've ever been.

When you can see your numbers changing over time, it will be easier to trust that your hard work is paying off. Some day, it will be a real mind-bender for you to look back on your first numbers and see how far you've come. Seeing visible evidence of your progress will help keep you motivated over the long-term.

Physical health   Week of_____ Week of_____ Week of_____
Sleeping
Appetite
Energy levels
Strength
Immunity
Resting heart rate

Emotional health
Connected to others
Ready to meet challenges
Overall happiness
Overall contentment
Guilt

Mental health
Worry or anxiety
Sadness
Loneliness
Overall engagement and excitement about life
Clear-headedness
Motivation levels
Work-life balance

Spiritual health
Feeling connected to a higher consciousness
Trusting in life
Spending time in a contemplative practice (whether praying or meditating)

Staying the Course

Many times, by the time people show up in my office, they have tried everything else—the antidepressants, the surgeries, the prescription drugs—and they still feel awful. Perhaps this is how you feel, too, and it's what drove you to read this book. As painful as it is to feel like you've exhausted your options, there is also something very powerful in that realization. It forces you to choose your own path, and then to trust it. I call it the gift of having no other options.

Whatever has brought you to this point in your health journey can be a catalyst for opening your mind and your heart to a new path—one that's customized to you, your likes, your needs, and your desires. Let it inspire you to do things differently than you've done before. And let it fuel you to keep going. You have nothing to lose and everything to gain.

When you are creating the conditions for wellness and listening to your inner wisdom, so much is possible: a stronger heart, a body that supports you, more meaningful work, more relaxation, better relationships, and hobbies that help you express your creativity. When you orient your life to better take care of your heart, your heart will take care of you. It's not just your health that improves, it's your *whole life*.

Now, the seed of your renewed heart is already in the ground. I can't say exactly when it is going to sprout, but I can promise you that you are going to be grateful to yourself for planting it. Keep watering it with your action. Keep trusting that it knows what to do. And get excited because something beautiful is preparing to bloom.

ACKNOWLEDGMENTS

I acknowledge with love:

- All the many teachers of all different forms who have shown up in my life at just the right time, believing in me and my ideas about holistic health and healing. Their encouragement and support in helping me expand these ideas and put them into action has in turn helped many people, including me.
- All the clients and students who have come into my counseling practice and yoga classes. I have learned so much from you, and am honored and grateful for the opportunity to work with you in such an intimate capacity. Your dedication and commitment to your healing process is truly inspiring!
- All the people behind the scenes who helped me put this book together. I am forever grateful for your time, dedication, and commitment to this project. You are all AMAZING.
- Without a connection to higher consciousness, I never would have found the path that has led me towards health, happiness, enlightenment, liberation, and release.

This book does not belong to me. I was only the vehicle for it to come into fruition in the perfect time and space. It originated from a source greater than me. I am grateful and honored to have played a role in its creation.

Namaste (which is the Sanskrit word that means, 'The divine light within me acknowledges the divine light within you').

NOTES

1. "Promoting Diversity in Neuroscience." *Nature Neuroscience* 21, no. 1 (2018). doi: 10.1038/s41593-017-0052-6.
2. "Women in Elective Office 2019." Center for American Women in Politics. http://www.cawp.rutgers.edu/women-elective-office-2019 (accessed January 25, 2019).
3. Ziegler, Katie. "Female Candidates Win in Historic Numbers." National Conference of State Legislators. November 8, 2018. http://www.ncsl.org/blog/2018/11/08/female-candidates-win-in-historic-numbers.aspx.
4. "Women Will Hold Record Numbers of Elected Offices in 2019. See Where They Made the Biggest Gains." The Center for Public Integrity. March 6, 2018. Updated December 19, 2018. https://publicintegrity.org/state-politics/share-of-women-in-elected-office-in-every-state/.
5. Saba, Jennifer. "Corporate America's Gender Gap: Few Women in the C-Suite." *The New York Times*. December 19, 2017. https://www.nytimes.com/2017/12/19/business/dealbook/corporate-americas-gender-gap.html.
6. "2018 Study on Sexual Harassment and Assault." Stop Street Harassment. February 21, 2018. http://www.stopstreetharassment.org/resources/2018-national-sexual-abuse-report/.
7. Liu, L., Sidani, J.E., Shensa, A., Radovic, A., Miller, E., Colditz, J.B., Primack, B.A. "Association Between Social Media Use and Depression Among U.S. Young Adults." *Depression and Anxiety* 33, no. 4 (2016). 323–331. doi: 10.1002/da.22466.
8. President and Fellows of Harvard College. "The State of the Nation's Housing." Joint Center for Housing Studies of Harvard University. 2017. http://www.jchs.harvard.edu/sites/default/files/harvard_jchs_state_of_the_nations_housing_2017.pdf.

9. Baio, J., Wiggins, L., Christensen, D.L., Maenner, M.J., Daniels, J., Warren, Z., Kurzius-Spencer, M., Zahorodny, et al. "Prevalence of Autism Spectrum Disorder Among Children Aged 8 Years—Autism and Developmental Disabilities Monitoring Network, 11 Sites, United States, 2014." *Surveillance Summaries* 67, no. 6 (2018). 1–23.
10. "Data and Statistics About ADHD." Centers for Disease Control and Prevention. https://www.cdc.gov/ncbddd/adhd/data.html (accessed February 25, 2019).
11. Amario, C.V., Ballal, M.L., Chey, W.D., Nordstrom, C., Khanna, D., Spiegel, B.M.R. "Burden of Gastrointestinal Symptoms in the United States: Results of a Nationally Representative Survey of over 71,000 Americans." *The American Journal of Gastroenterology* 113, no. 1 (2018). 1701–1710. doi: 10.1038/s41395-018-0256-8.
12. "Body Mass Index (BMI)." Center for Disease Control and Prevention. Updated May 15, 2015. https://www.cdc.gov/healthyweight/assessing/bmi/ (accessed February 19, 2019).
13. Neary, N.M., Booker, O.J., Abel, B.S., Matta, J.R., Muldoon, N., Sinaii, N., Pettigrew, R.I., et al. "Hypercortisolism is Associated with Increased Coronary Arterial Atherosclerosis: Analysis of Noninvasive Coronary Angiography Using Multidetector Computerized Tomography." *Journal of Clinical Endocrinology and Metabolism* 98, no. 5 (2013). 2045–2052. doi: 10.1210/jc.2012-375.
14. Jackson, S.E., Kirschbaum, C., Steptoe, A. "Hair Cortisol and Adiposity in a Population-Based Sample of 2,527 Men and Women Aged 54 to 87 Years." *Obesity* 25, no. 3 (2017). 539–544. doi: 10.1002/oby.21733.
15. "Assessing Your Weight and Health Risk." National Heart, Lung, and Blood Institute. https://www.nhlbi.nih.gov/health/educational/lose_wt/risk.htm (accessed February 1, 2019).
16. McSweeney, J.C. "Women's Early Warning Symptoms of Acute Myocardial Infarction." *Circulation* 108 (2003). 2619–2623. doi: 10.1161/01.CIR.0000097116.29625.7C.
17. Buckley, T., Soo Hoo, S.Y., Fethney, J., Shaw, E., Hanson, P.S., Tofler, G.H. "Triggering of Acute Coronary Occlusion by Episodes

of Anger." *European Heart Journal: Acute Cardiovascular Care* 4, no. 6 (2015). doi: 10.1177/2048872615568969.
18. "What Is Depression?" The American Psychiatric Association. https://www.psychiatry.org/patients-families/depression/what-is-depression (accessed February 19, 2019).
19. Jackson, C.A., Sudlow, C.L.M., and Mishra, G.D. "Psychological Distress and Risk of Myocardial Infarction and Stroke in the 45 and Up Study." *Circulation: Cardiovascular Quality and Outcomes* 11, no. 9 (2018). doi: 10.1161/CIRCOUTCOMES.117.004500.
20. Kessler, R.C., McGonagle, K.A., Swartz, M., Blazer, D.G., Nelson, C.B. "Sex and Depression in the National Comorbidity Survey. I: Lifetime Prevalence, Chronicity and Recurrence." *Journal of Affective Disorders* 29, no. 2–3 (1993). 85–96. doi: 10.1016/0165-0327(93)90026-G.
21. Pan, A., Okereke, O.I., Sun, Q., Logroscino, G., Manson, J.E., Willett, W.C., Ascherio, A., et al. "Depression and Incident Stroke in Women." *Stroke* 42, no. 10 (2011). 2770–2775. doi: 10.1161/STROKEAHA.111.617043.
22. Schnatz, P.F., Nudy, M., Shively, C.A., Powell, A., O'Sullivan, D.M. "A Prospective Analysis of the Association Between Cardiovascular Disease and Depression in Middle-Aged Women." *Menopause* 18, no. 10 (2011). 1096–1100. doi: 10.1097/gme.0b013e3182184928.
23. Clapp, M., Aurora, N., Herrera, L., Bhatia, M., Wilen, E., and Wakefield, S. "Gut Microbiota's Effect on Mental Health: The Gut-Brain Axis." *Clinics and Practice* 7, no. 4 (2017). 987. doi: 10.4081/cp.2017.987.
24. Sofi, F., et al. "Adherence to Mediterranean Diet and Health Status: Meta-analysis." *BMJ (Clinical Research Edition)* 337, no. a1344 (September 11, 2008). doi: 10.1136/bmj.a1344.
25. Rosanoff, A., Weaver, C.M., Rude, R.K. "Suboptimal Magnesium Status in the United States: Are the Health Consequences Underestimated?" *Nutrition Reviews* 70, no. 3 (2012). 153–164. doi: 10.1111/j.1753-4887.2011.00465.
26. Simon, H.B. "Exercise and Health: Dose and Response, Considering Both Ends of the Curve." *The American Journal of Medicine* 128, no. 11 (2015). 1171–1177. doi: 10.1016/j.amjmed.2015.05.012.

27. Chu, P., Gotink, R.A., Yeh, G.Y., Goldie, S.J., Hunink, M.G. "The effectiveness of yoga in modifying risk factors for cardiovascular disease and metabolic syndrome: A systematic review and meta-analysis of randomized controlled trials." *European Journal of Preventive Cardiology* 3, no. 23 (2016). 291–307. doi: 10.1177/2047487314562741.
28. May, R., Sanchez-Gonzalez, M., Dillon, K., Batchelor, W., and Fincham, F. "Effect of Anger and Trait Forgiveness on Cardiovascular Risk in Young Adult Females." *The American Journal of Cardiology* 114 (2014). doi: 10.1016/j.amjcard.2014.04.007.
29. Lawler, K.A., Younger, J.W., Piferi, R.L., Billington, E., Jobe, R., Edmondson, K., and Jones, W.H. "A Change of Heart: Cardiovascular Correlates of Forgiveness in Response to Interpersonal Conflict." *Journal of Behavioral Medicine* 26, no. 5 (2003). 373–393.
30. Hannon, P., Finkel, E.J., Kumashiro, M., and Rusbult, C.E. "The Soothing Effects of Forgiveness on Victims' and Perpetrators' Blood Pressure." *Personal Relationships* (2011). doi: 10.1111/j.1475-6811.2011.01356.x.
31. Carson, J., Keefe, Francis, G., Veeraindar, M.F., Lynch, T., Thorp, S., and Buechler, J.L. "Forgiveness and Chronic Low Back Pain: A Preliminary Study Examining the Relationship of Forgiveness to Pain, Anger, and Psychological Distress." *The Journal of Pain: Official Journal of the American Pain Society* 6 (2005). 84–91. doi: 10.1016/j.jpain.2004.10.012.
32. Toussaint, L.L., Shields, G.S., Slavich, G.M. "Forgiveness, Stress, and Health: A 5-Week Dynamic Parallel Process Study." *Annals of Behavioral Medicine* 50, no. 5 (2016). 727–735.
33. Rosenkranz, M., Davidson, R.J., MacGoon, D.G., Sheridan, J.F., Kalin, N.H., Lutz, A. "A Comparison of Mindfulness-Based Stress Reduction and an Active Control in Modulation of Neurogenic Inflammation." *Brain, Behavior, and Immunity* 27 (2013). 174–184. doi: 10.1016/j.bbi.2012.10.013.
34. Carmody, J., Baer, R. "Relationships Between Mindfulness Practice and Levels of Mindfulness, Medical and Psychological Symptoms and Well-Being in a Mindfulness-Based Stress Reduction Program." *Journal of Behavioral Medicine* 31, no. 1 (2008). doi: 10.1007/s10865-007-9130-7.

35. Miller, J.J., Fletcher, K., Kabat-Zinn, J. "Three-year Follow-up and Clinical Implications of Mindfulness Meditation-Based Stress Reduction Intervention in the Treatment of Anxiety Disorders." *General Hospital Psychiatry* 17, no. 3 (1995). 192–200. doi: 10.1016/0163-8343(95)00025-M.
36. Creswell, J.D., Irwin, M.R., Burklund, L.J., et al. "Mindfulness-Based Stress Reduction Training Reduces Loneliness and Pro-inflammatory Gene Expression in Older Adults: a Small Randomized Controlled Trial." *Brain, Behavior, and Immunity* 26, no. 7 (2012). 1095–101. doi: 10.1016/j.bbi.2012.07.006.
37. Greenberg, J., Reiner, K., Meiran, N. "Mind the Trap: Mindfulness Practice Reduces Cognitive Rigidity." *Plos One* 7, no. 5. (2012). doi: 10.1371/journal.pone.0036206.
38. Zeidan, F., Johnson, S.K., Diamond, B.J., David, Z., Goolkasian, P. "Mindfulness Meditation Improves Cognition: Evidence of Brief Mental Training." *Consciousness and Cognition* 19, no. 2 (2010). 597–605. doi: 10.1016/j.concog.2010.03.014.
39. Katterman, S.N., Kleinman, B.M., Hood, M.M., Nackers, L.M., Corsica, J.A. "Mindfulness Meditation as an Intervention for Binge Eating, Emotional Eating, and Weight Loss: A Systematic Review." *Eating Behaviors* 15, no. 2 (2014). 197–204. doi: 10.1016/j.eatbeh.2014.01.00.
40. Martires, J., Zeidler, M. "The Value of Mindfulness Meditation in the Treatment of Insomnia." *Current Opinion in Pulmonary Medicine* 21, no. 6 (2015). 547–552. doi: 10.1097/MCP.0000000000000207.
41. Goyal, M., Singh, S., Sibinga, E.M., et al. "Meditation Programs for Psychological Stress and Well-being: a Systematic Review and Meta-analysis." *JAMA Internal Medicine* 174, no. 3 (2014). 357–368. doi: 10.1001/jamainternmed.2013.13018.
42. Koike, M.K., Cardoso, R. "Meditation Can Produce Beneficial Effects to Prevent Cardiovascular Disease." *Hormone Molecular Biology and Clinical Investigation* 18, no. 3 (2014). 137–143. doi: 10.1515/hmbci-2013-0056.

www.ingramcontent.com/pod-product-compliance
Lightning Source LLC
Chambersburg PA
CBHW071710020426
42333CB00017B/2208